Who Was Jesus?

Other books by Hendrikus Boers

Theology Out of the Ghetto
What Is New Testament Christology?
Neither on This Mountain nor in Jerusalem

Who Was Jesus?

*The Historical Jesus
and the Synoptic Gospels*

Hendrikus Boers

1817

Harper & Row, Publishers, San Francisco

New York, Grand Rapids, Philadelphia, St. Louis
London, Singapore, Sydney, Tokyo

FIRST EDITION

Library of Congress Cataloging-in-Publication Data

Boers, Hendrikus.
  Who Was Jesus?

  1. Jesus Christ—History of doctrines—Early church,
ca. 30–600.   2. Bible. N.T. Gospels—Criticism,
interpretation, etc.   I. Title.
BT198.B62   1989   226'.06   88-46004
ISBN 0–06–060809–9

89   90   91   92   93   HC   10   9   8   7   6   5   4   3   2   1

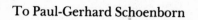
To Paul-Gerhard Schoenborn

Contents

Acknowledgments

This volume is the result of an engagement with the subject matter of the Christian Gospels in courses for theology students over a period of more than a decade. From the first time I taught a course on the subject to the most recent repetition of it, I have benefited greatly from the critical comments and even corrections contributed by students in those courses over the years. They know that they deserve recognition—many will discover formulations to which they contributed directly—and I am glad to acknowledge my debt to them here. I also thank my former colleague and longtime friend, Jack Sanders, for his encouragement and helpful suggestions during the early stages of the work.

Special thanks are due to former graduate student, now colleague, Gail O'Day, for invaluable editorial help in an earlier version of this work, and to John Cook, also a former graduate student, for his many hours of bibliographic research.

In dedicating this volume to Paul-Gerhard Schoenborn I honor a friend whose gentle but determined dedication to the happiness and dignity of every human being came to mind many times over the years. As I worked on this study, I remembered also those occasions when, together with his wife Margaret and my wife Ida, we were able to appreciate that life was worth living. That too is what this book is about.

Hendrikus Boers
Emory University

The Crucifixion of Christ by Matthias Grünewald. Used by permission of Musée d'Unterlinden, Colmar, France. Photograph by O. Zimmermann.

Introduction

In Matthias Grünewald's famous painting of Jesus on the cross John the Baptist stands firmly on the earth, pointing with an exaggerated forefinger to the crucified Jesus in a gesture that says, "There is the Lamb of God who takes away the sins of the world" (John 1:29). The inscription behind John, "Illum oportet crescere, me autem minui," refers to another verse in the Fourth Gospel: "He must increase, and I diminish" (John 3:30). Grünewald's highly christological interpretation of Jesus is the point of departure for the present study. It is the way Christians have reacted to Jesus through the ages, beginning with the traditions on which the first three Gospels are based.

But what did Jesus think of himself? The first, main, part of this study ends with the conclusion that the situation is the direct inverse of Grünewald's great interpretation. Jesus interpreted the significance of his activity by pointing to John as the decisive figure whose presence marked the coming of God's kingdom. "What did you go out to see in the desert? A reed swaying in the wind? No? What then did you go out looking for? A man dressed in fine clothing? Look, persons who wear finery live in palaces! So what did you go out for? To see a prophet? Indeed, I tell you, he is more than a prophet. He is the one concerning whom it is written, 'Behold, I send my messenger before me.' In fact, no one born on earth [literally, "of a woman"] is greater than John the Baptist, for all the prophets and the Law prophesied until John the Baptist. If you are willing to accept this, he is the expected Elijah" (Matt. 11:7–14, without the christologizing features).

Who was the expected Elijah, and what was his significance? In Malachi 4:5 the prophet writes, "Behold, I send you the prophet Elijah before the great, the awesome, day of the Lord's arrival," and in 3:1, speaking in the name of God, "Behold, I send my messenger before me; he will prepare the way for me." The expected Elijah was obviously the one who was to initiate God's own coming to his people. Thus it is not surprising that we read in Luke 16:16, "The Law and the prophets are until John; from then on the kingdom of God is proclaimed." As the returning Elijah, John marked the turn of the ages. He was the final, **eschatological** figure before the coming of God's kingdom. Jesus lived in the awareness that the kingdom of God had been initiated by the return of Elijah in the person of John. When Jesus pointed to John as the decisive eschatological figure he revealed that he understood himself to be living in a time when the kingdom of God had already arrived. By pointing not to himself but to John the Baptist, and by emphasizing John's significance, Jesus also disclosed his own significance as one who already enjoyed the presence of the kingdom of God.

In a reply to a question from John, which we now have only in a highly Christianized form in Matthew 11:3 (only Jesus' answer, not the present form of John's question, interests us here), Jesus formulates his position very clearly: "Go and tell John what you hear and see: The blind see and the lame walk, lepers are healed and the deaf hear and the dead are resurrected and to the poor good tidings are proclaimed. And blessed is everyone who is not scandalized by me" (Matt. 11:4–6). Jesus evidently believed that the kingdom of God had actually arrived. But why would anyone be scandalized by him?

The answer to that question is to be found in his behavior, which, especially in contrast with that of John, was disgraceful. And yet, paradoxically, it was only in relationship to John that his conduct was understandable. Jesus' statement of this paradox is recorded in the tradition of Matt. 11:18–19, "John came and he neither ate nor drank, and they said, 'He has a demon.' I came eating and drinking, and they said, 'Look, what a glutton and a boozer; a friend of publicans and sinners.' " John was an ascetic; Jesus behaved like a man of the world. John withdrew from a world of sin into the desert in order to prepare himself and his followers for God's coming; Jesus indulged in the pleasures of that same sinful world, associating with the very types of people from whom John expected a radical change. Yet Jesus found justification for his own behavior precisely by seeing it as coordinate with that of John. According to another passage (Matt. 21:23–27), when challenged to explain the basis of his authority, Jesus answered in a typically rabbinic manner by means of a counterquestion in which he appealed to the authority of John's activity as the basis for his own, "If you tell me on what authority John baptized, you will have your answer!" Early Christians, unable to understand how Jesus could explain his own authority by an appeal to that of John the Baptist, interpreted Jesus' reply as a way of tricking his questioners into accepting his refusal to answer (cf. vv. 25–27).

John the Baptist's importance for understanding the significance of Jesus was not a presupposition of the present study but rather a conclusion that had not been anticipated when it was started. The study was motivated by a double skepticism: (1) whether one could establish anything of significance about Jesus that could be considered historically reliable even if only within the limits of probability set by critical historical inquiry, and (2) whether the results of such an inquiry could contribute anything of real value for the understanding of Jesus or of the Christian religion. The primary purpose was not to see what could be established historically about Jesus, but to try to account for the history of the traditions used by the evangelists in the writing of the first three, or **synoptic Gospels**. That a rather distinct picture of Jesus did emerge is thus not the fulfillment of the expectations of the study but a conclusion that was called for by the investigation of the material. The nature of the material itself determined that the study eventually became a "search for the historical Jesus"; the events in the life of Jesus were, after all, the most important factors in explaining the history of the traditions on which the Gospels were based. At certain points it also became necessary to use information from the Fourth Gospel to answer questions not only about Jesus, but also about the history of some of the synoptic traditions. The end results, then, were not my initial goals. They came, so to speak, as challenges to my double skepticism.

What emerged is the powerful story of a young man of relatively comfortable circumstances from Nazareth who, through deep religious commitment, gave up a comfortable life to become a disciple of John the Baptist, a desert preacher, by whom he was baptized, which signified his purification from sin and turning away from a sinful world. However, as we encounter him in the Gospels at the prime of his life, he is back in the world from which he had turned away under the influence of John. We find him associating, not with the pious, but with sinners, harlots, and publicans, which he justifies with the claim of doing so as a sign that the kingdom of God had arrived where it was least expected, among the religious and social outcasts.

His life ended with one of the most gruesome deaths in antiquity, execution by crucifixion at the hands of the Roman authorities. He had been handed over as a messianic pretender by the Jewish leaders, not because of religious envy, but because they feared that he might have led an uprising against Rome, which would inevitably have been oppressed with brutality. Jesus may never have been a messianic pretender, but there is incontrovertible evidence that some of his followers did understand him in that way, which must have contributed to the deep concern for the well-being of their people among the Jewish leaders and probably provided the brutal procurator Pontius Pilate with evidence for the conviction of Jesus. That his followers were armed when he was arrested in Gethsemane makes it difficult to deny with certainty that he himself had become involved in armed resistance against the Romans.

The investigation of the Gospel materials insofar as they relate to the life of Jesus provides insight into who he was but not a clear understanding of his significance. That understanding emerges also for his followers only after his death. Whereas the death of other messianic pretenders meant the end of their movements, the movement that had gathered around Jesus grew into one of the greatest religions of the world. His death on the cross shattered all the political messianic hopes that some of his followers had cherished. What survived his crucifixion was a different kind of impression from that of a political messiah. It is the impression that is preserved in the synoptic Gospels. Jesus did not die on the cross as a martyr for his cause on behalf of the religious and social outcasts, but as a messianic pretender. But his death did make of him more than a teacher; he became a symbol, the symbol for what his life with the religious and social outcasts had meant. And so even though he did not die as a martyr for the cause of the outcasts of society, by becoming a symbol for that cause, his death, ironically, did take on the meaning of a martyrdom, of a *martyrium*, a witness through suffering and death, for that cause which Christianity in its most noble form has represented throughout its history.

Our task will be to try, on the one hand, to discern the facts of his life through historical inquiry but, on the other, to remain aware that his meaning is not recognizable through such an investigation. And so, as we become aware of those facts, we may expect to become even more aware of the significance that he had for his followers, a significance that could not be expressed in factual terms.

It is my hope that all readers who are committed to the pursuit of truth—Christians and Jews as well as atheists and skeptics—may profit from this book. Readers who have the greatest stake in it are obviously Christians because an essential feature of the Christian faith is that its foundation rests in the life of Jesus. Faith for the modern believer precedes historical knowledge of the facts of the life of Jesus; it would be difficult, if not impossible, to find someone who was led to faith in Christ after, and on the basis of, first establishing the facts about the life of Jesus by purely historical inquiry. Faith's self-understanding that it is based on the facts of the life of Jesus is not the result of historical inquiry but a presupposition of faith itself; it is a postulate of Christian faith, not a product of historical inquiry.

Even though historical inquiry is as incapable as faith of presenting the facts of the life of Jesus as they actually happened, that does not mean that historical inquiry and faith are the same. From a historical point of view it would be a mistake to say that the perspective of faith is as good as that of historical inquiry, but it would be equally wrong to say that the perspective of the historian is as good as (or even better than!) that of faith when it concerns matters of faith. That neither can be "objective" does not make them one of a kind. The confusion of these two perspectives is rooted in the postulate of Christian faith mentioned above, that it understands itself to be based on the facts of the life of Jesus understood "historically," that is, that they actually happened. These same facts can also come into view as the objects of historical inquiry. The facts themselves, however, remain beyond the reach of our understanding, and so we are left only with the two perspectives on them, each presenting them in its own way. This confusion is compounded when each of these perspectives claims to be better capable of answering the questions of the other, thus substituting the one for the other. At the most fundamental level this occurs when faith mistakes its postulate of being based on the facts of the life of Jesus for a historical proposition. The confusion of the two perspectives, and the resulting conflict between them, is one of the most serious, if not the most serious, problems for contemporary Christian theology.

All of this, however, does not mean that the historical question is irrelevant to faith. It is crucially important to the self-understanding of faith that historical inquiry confirms faith's grounding in the facts of the life of Jesus. The problem is that at many points historical inquiry contradicts the historicity of the Gospel accounts on which faith is based. That does not have to challenge the Christian faith itself, but it does challenge faith's self-understanding. In this regard an inquiry such as the present one could be valuable for faith by forcing it to reflect on its own self-understanding. To begin with, the inquiry will show that faith's perspective on the facts of the life of Jesus is not the same as that of historical reasoning. More importantly, by uncovering the contradictions between the presuppositions of faith and the results of historical inquiry it will provide a context in which faith can reflect on the nature of its own presuppositions. For that reason the inquiry does not move only from the life of Jesus as it is presented in the Gospels to an understanding that results from historical inquiry; in a second part it also traces the development from the life of Jesus to the emergence of faith in him as the Christ. In this second part the perspectives of faith and historical understanding are not opposed to one another. Rather, historical inquiry functions as an attempt to understand the Christian faith in its origins, as a type of "critique of the reason of faith," similar to Immanuel Kant's attempt to understand how theoretical reasoning functions in his *Critique of Pure Reason*.

Even though this study has also become a search for the historical Jesus, its primary purpose remains to introduce the reader to the history of the synoptic traditions. The discussion of the various Gospel traditions never becomes subservient to what has become its second purpose, namely, to answer the question, Who was Jesus? The history of the traditions and the way they were used in the Gospels continue to be discussed for their own sake, to maintain not only the primary purpose of the study but also a maximum degree of impartiality in the attempt to discover who Jesus was. This is not a study of the life of Jesus for which appeal is made to the Gospel materials, but a study of the Gospel materials from which a picture of the life of Jesus emerges.

It should be pointed out, however, that although the fundamental purpose of the present study is to enable the reader to become comfortable with the treatment of the synoptic traditions from the perspective of their historical developments, there is also another way of looking at this same material. One can start from the perspective of the Gospels themselves, for which the traditions constituted the basic material, plied and molded into unified compositions. From that perspective the Gospels are to be read as integral units, not piecemeal as we are doing here.

This volume is not an introduction to current New Testament scholarship but to the history of the traditions about Jesus on which the synoptic Gospels are based, from a historical point of view. For readers familiar with the history of Jesus research it may be helpful if I indicate how my study relates to some of the more recent work. As the title indicates, in *Jesus and the Word* (New York: Scribner's, 1958) Rudolf Bultmann focused purely on the teaching of Jesus. He was convinced that scholarship had no access to the original teaching itself but had to satisfy itself with the teaching as it was remembered in the earliest layers of the tradition. Bultmann also did not believe that one could know anything of the actual life of Jesus with historical certainty, and he did not think that that mattered for an understanding of the Christian faith.

As part of the so-called new quest of the historical Jesus, Günther Bornkamm, in *Jesus of Nazareth* (New York: Harper Bros., 1960), while following Bultmann in many respects, tried to uncover some of the facts of the life of Jesus, especially the significance of the person of Jesus for his proclamation. Notwithstanding these differences, both Bultmann and Bornkamm tried to go as far back to Jesus as possible. In the present study I investigate all the layers of material without attaching greater value to the older layers. I consider the entire tradition as important for understanding who Jesus was; indeed, his real meaning became clear to his followers only after his death. The development of the tradition was the way in which that meaning came to expression.

In this study no prior knowledge of New Testament methods of inquiry is required of the reader. As far as possible, methodological questions are raised as they come up in the investigation of the material itself. All that is required of the reader is that she or he has available a synopsis of the Gospels. I worked with Kurt Aland's *Synopsis quattuor evangeliorum* (Stuttgart: Württembergische Bibelanstalt, 1964). It is also available with parallel English translations under the title *Synopsis of the Four Gospels* and in English only as *Synopsis of the Four Gospels, English Edition*. I recommend any one of these to the reader, but any text with the Gospels in parallel will serve the purpose. To assist the reader, section headings in the *Synopsis* are indicated by # followed by the section number. All quotations are translated from the Greek and will frequently not agree in every detail with translations. The reader may find useful Rudolf Bultmann's *The History of the Synoptic Tradition* (New York: Harper & Row, 1968), although it is rather technical for the beginner.

I strongly urge the reader to read the Gospel passages indicated in the headings of the various sections before reading the sections themselves, even if she or he is familiar with the passages. Although this may seem an additional burden, rereading the passages makes it much easier to follow the discussions.

One assumption of Gospel research should be presented here at the outset: in a general way, and with great caution, the study proceeds on the widely accepted view that Mark is the oldest Gospel and that Matthew and Luke, independent of each other, used Mark as one of their sources. In addition, Matthew and Luke used a second common source, generally referred to as Q, from the German *Quelle*, meaning simply "source." Whether such a source actually existed remains a question of informed speculation. I use Q here for that common material, without assuming an actual common source: Q material rather than a source Q. Furthermore, Matthew and Luke each independently used yet other sources. It is safe to assume that neither Matthew nor Luke felt obliged to reproduce their sources verbally exactly as they found them. They undoubtedly knew a large part of the tradition in more than one version, written and oral, and they reproduced each tradition in the way they considered most reliable or appropriate.

For material that occurs in Mark, I refer always to chapter and verse of that Gospel followed by //s if the passage also occurs in both Matthew and Luke, for example, Mark 14:53–65, //s. Where only one parallel occurs, reference will be to Mark, //, irrespective of whether the parallel is in Matthew or Luke. I assume readers will be able to find the parallel in their Gospel parallel texts. Reference to Q material in Matthew and Luke will be to either Matthew // or Luke, //, *usually* depending on which is considered to be closer to the original.

The first occurrence of a few inevitable technical terms are in boldface print. They are explained in a glossary at the end of the volume.

Who Was Jesus?

Part 1

JESUS THE MESSIAH

Thus the community embellished and wove the life image of their master. But they did more than that; they preserved in it . . . a good piece of the authentic and original life.

WILHELM BOUSSET

CHAPTER 1

The Birth and Messiahship of Jesus

A good place to begin our investigation is the reception of Jesus in Nazareth (Mark 6:1–6a, //s) and the stories of the birth and infancy in the first chapters of Matthew and Luke. The contrast between these reveals what is at issue in a figure such as Jesus. According to the story of the reception of Jesus in Nazareth, the persons who had the kind of knowledge about him that would be of interest to the historian said, "Isn't this the son of the carpenter, the son of Mary, whose brothers are James and Joses and Judah and Simon, and are his sisters not here with us?" On the basis of that knowledge they were scandalized by him!

By contrast, the stories of his birth and infancy are legends that cannot be used for historical inquiry concerning the events they portray. And yet those legends express more accurately who Jesus was than the precise historical knowledge of the villagers of Nazareth. The real meaning of Jesus for those who followed him and believed in him escaped those who had precise knowledge of the historical facts about him but came to expression in the symbolic accounts of his birth and infancy. In that regard the legends too are historical, but in another sense. They provide us with historical knowledge of the meaning that Jesus had for his followers and for those who believed in him, a knowledge that was not available to those who depended on knowledge of historical facts about him. This does not suggest a privileged estimation of Jesus. The real meaning of persons rarely depend on knowledge of concrete "historical" facts about them.

We now turn our attention, first, to the failure to recognize Jesus as a significant figure in the story of his reception in Nazareth, and then to the symbolic expression of his meaning in the legends of his birth and infancy.

3

A. THE RECEPTION IN NAZARETH (MARK 6:1–6a, //s; #139, cf. #33)

The three versions of the story of the reception of Jesus in Nazareth provide an excellent introduction to the ways in which tradition is incorporated into the Gospels. Tensions in the story in Mark suggest that Mark may have combined two partly conflicting traditions in his version. The Matthean version displays Matthew's excellent editorial ability in handling Markan material; by small changes he smoothed out the tension in the Markan version. The Lukan version reveals such extensive differences that one might consider him having drawn from a different tradition of the story. The fact, however, that the same tension is still evident in his version suggests that he too probably edited the Markan version of the tradition but far more extensively than Matthew.

The Lukan version also reveals something else about the use of traditions in the composition of the Gospels. What Luke expresses in the passage is very different from what the text says in Mark and in Matthew. Whereas the villagers of Nazareth were scandalized by their familiarity with Jesus in Mark and Matthew, Luke has given the story a powerful christological meaning, among other things, by introducing quotations from Scripture as the essence of Jesus' teaching in the synagogue (vv. 18–19). Even though Luke retains the proverb of the prophet who is rejected by his own people, the reason for the rejection of Jesus in Nazareth in his version of the story has shifted from the people's familiarity with Jesus to the messianic claim that he made in his synagogue speech.

The flow in the Markan version of the story of Jesus' reception in Nazareth is noteworthy. Reaction to Jesus is positive at first (v. 2), but by the end of verse 3 "they were scandalized by him." The bridge between these two reactions—the first part of verse 3—is ambiguous. From the perspective of verse 2 the fact that the people of Nazareth knew Jesus and his family enhances their amazement at his outstanding ability. The final statement in verse 3, however, looking back at the same material, interprets that knowledge as the reason for their being scandalized by him. This change in attitude could be the product of a skillful writing technique of the author. Or the reaction of the people of Nazareth could actually have changed from original enthusiasm to rejection, so that the passage represents in brief a development that took place over a longer period of time. However, the contradiction between the impression Jesus' miracles made on the Nazarene villagers in the first part, "*Such miracles that happen through his hands!*" (v. 2), and his inability to perform miracles in Nazareth in the second part, "he was unable to perform a *single* miracle there" (v. 5), suggests that Mark probably combined two contradictory traditions. The crudeness of the formulation of verse 5 supports this impression. The text first states that Jesus was unable to perform "a single miracle" there but then corrects the statement, seemingly in view of verse 2, according to which he must have performed miracles in Nazareth, "except that he healed a few sick persons by laying hands on them."

The point of the story in Mark is made clear by means of the proverb quoted in verse 4, "A prophet is not without honor except in his fatherland," further clarified by the comments in verses 5–6. The proverb with its clarification that Jesus was unable to perform any miracles in Nazareth reminds one of a double proverb attributed to Jesus in the **Oxyrhynchus Papyrus 1.5**, "A prophet is not welcome in his country; neither does a physician practice healing on his acquaintances." The parallel in Luke is more complete with the addition of "physician heal yourself" in verse 23. The point made by the proverb does not fit the first part of the scene in which the people react positively to Jesus (Mark 6:2), but it does fit the negative interpretation that they were scandalized by him at the end of verse 3 in the second part. A tradition also exists that Jesus' own family was so scandalized by him that they considered him insane (Mark 3:20–21, 31–35, //s). We will discuss that tradition later.

Matthew made relatively minor, but typically skillful, editorial changes in the story. He smoothed out Mark's clumsy formulation, "And he was unable to perform a single miracle there, except to heal a few sick persons by laying hands on them" (Mark 6:5–6), which, as we have already seen, contradicts "*such miracles* that happen through his hands!" in 6:2. Skillfully Matthew reformulated, "And he did not do *many* miracles there because of their disbelief" (Matt. 13:58). In this way Matthew eliminated not only the contradiction of Mark 6:2 (cf. Matt. 13:54), but also the reference to Jesus' *inability* to perform miracles in Nazareth, which must have been theologically inconceivable for Matthew. According to him, it was not due to inability that Jesus performed only a few miracles in Nazareth, but through his own choice.

Luke's version of the story is so different that perhaps he used a different source. However, the same tension between amazed enthusiasm— "everyone witnessed concerning him, and they were amazed by the kind words that came from his mouth" (v. 22)—and the now even harsher rejection of Jesus (vv. 23–30) is also present in his version of the story, suggesting that he too probably depended on Mark. Oral tradition would hardly have preserved such a tension in a single source.

In Luke's version it is in Jesus' own response in verses 23–24, not in a statement about the reaction of the people of Nazareth, that the reader learns that "they were scandalized by him" (Mark 6:3), which makes initially clear that he was not well received. The question "is he not the son of Joseph?" (v. 22) does not have to be negative, although it was probably christologically negative for Luke. It is the only element of the presentation of Jesus' family relationships that Luke retains, made into an explicit reference to Joseph. The villagers of Nazareth failed to recognize that God, not Joseph, was Jesus' father. We encounter a similar lack of understanding in Mary when, as an understandably worried mother, she tells Jesus who had been left behind in Jerusalem, "Child, why do you treat us like this? Your father and I have sought you in anguish!" (2:48). Jesus replies, "Why is it that you look for me? Do you not realize that I have to be about my father's business?" (v. 49), correcting his mother's mistaken understanding of who his father is.

In Luke the proverb expressing Jesus' rejection at Nazareth, alluded to by all three accounts, no longer interprets the meaning of the incident to which the story refers. As we shall see, for Luke, rather than being interpreted by the proverb, the incident is a symbolic enactment of its meaning in a much larger context. That he preserved the allusion to the proverb in this new sense is a further indication that he probably depended on Mark. The point of the story in Luke is not that Jesus was rejected in Nazareth because the people from his hometown were too familiar with him (even if nothing contradicts that fact), but that he was rejected because of his messianic claim. Luke gave the story an explicitly christological meaning by having Jesus quote material from Scripture (Isa. 61:1–2, 58:6; cf. Luke 4:18–19) and claiming that those prophecies were fulfilled in him (v. 21). Seen in the light of this claim, the people's reaction amounted to a failure to recognize christologically who Jesus was. In Luke, the story has become the model for Israel's rejection of Christ, as the examples from Israel's past history reveal (vv. 25–27).

An interesting feature in Luke is that the miracles in Capernaum referred to in verse 23 had not yet been performed at this stage of Jesus' activity. His move to Capernaum is reported in Luke only in 4:31–32, upon which follow the miracles referred to in 4:23 (cf. 4:33–41). The reversed chronological sequence of events does not seem to have caught Luke's attention. The contrast between Jesus' rejection in Nazareth and the appreciation with which he was received in Capernaum (cf. esp. 4:42–43) is what interested him. Indeed, it was precisely Jesus' rejection in Nazareth (cf. vv. 28–30) that prompted his move to Capernaum, according to verses 31–32. This sequence is the model for Paul (and Barnabas) going to the Gentiles after they are rejected by the Jews, as Paul states in Acts 13:46, "Since you reject [the word of God] and do not consider yourselves worthy of eternal life, look, we turn to the Gentiles" (cf. also 18:6). Nazareth here symbolizes an unwilling Israel and Capernaum the responsive Gentiles. This symbolism is clarified in Jesus' statements in verses 25–27, referring to Gentiles having precedence over Jews.

The same motif is present in Luke's version of the parable of the banquet (14:15–24); after the original guests (Israel) reject the invitation to the banquet, the servants are sent first to the streets of the village (representing the outcasts of Jewish society) and then to the lanes and highways outside the city (representing the Gentiles) to invite whomever they can find (vv. 21–23). The parable of the banquet reveals that in Luke's view Israel as a whole did not reject Christ. The invitation to the Gentiles, those whom the servant had to call from beyond the limits of the city (v. 23), was made after the underprivileged in Israel had already responded positively to the invitation, as symbolized by the instructions to the servant: "Go to the streets and the lanes of the city, and bring here the poor and the maimed and the blind and the lame" (v. 21).

With regard to the present story readers should note that life had not always been rosy in Capernaum either, as Matthew 11:20–24 and Luke 10:15 indicate.

Luke places the story earlier in his Gospel (compare #33 with #139), almost immediately after the story of the temptation (4:1–13), with only general statements about his move to and work in Galilee in between (vv. 14–15). This may explain the inverted chronological sequence of the miracles that were supposed to have already taken place in Capernaum at the time of the present story when, according to verse 23, they were still in the future (cf. 4:33–41). Luke's editing of the story may have been complete before he moved it forward in his Gospel. In the story's original location, following the story of Jairus's daughter and the woman with a hemorrhage (Luke 8:40–56), where Mark and Matthew still have it, the reference to miracles in Capernaum would have appeared in the chronologically correct order. Luke may not have noticed that when he moved the story up to its present location the chronological order became reversed.

By moving the story with its present symbolic meaning forward as far as possible in his Gospel, Luke used it to signal to the reader the meaning of the gospel he was about to present. In Mark and Luke it is an incident of some significance in the life of Jesus. But for Luke it is of decisive importance, symbolizing in a powerful way the meaning of his entire Gospel, the rejection of Jesus by his people, in which the foundation is laid for the future movement of the gospel to the Gentiles as presented in his second book, the Acts of the Apostles.

Conclusion. The ability to perform miracles plays an important role in this story as told by all three evangelists. If Jesus performed miracles, as he probably did, he would have been recognized as an outstanding religious figure but by no means unique. The appearance of miracle workers was widespread in the entire Greco-Roman world, including Palestine. The closest counterparts were Galilean *hasidim* (holy men, charismatics) such as Hanina ben Dosa and Honi the Circle Drawer (both from the first century A.D.), famed for their sincere but unconventional piety (very similar to that of Jesus) and their ability to work miracles. Jesus may have assembled followers around him through his activity as a miracle worker, but even then his significance would almost certainly not have been limited to that of a miracle worker, which is also true of figures such as Hanina and Honi. Some around him may have been most impressed by Jesus' ability to perform miracles, but the performance of miracles was not the most central feature remembered about him in early Christianity. Neither were Hanina and Honi remembered primarily as miracle workers.

The story of Jesus' rejection in Nazareth as reported in Mark and Matthew reveals that the identity of Jesus could not be derived from knowledge of the facts of his life. People of Nazareth who were familiar with those facts were scandalized by him. Luke heightened the meaning of the story into a rejection of Jesus because of his implied messianic claim, and by placing it early in his narrative of the life of Jesus he signaled to his readers the meaning he saw in the story of Jesus. That Jesus was the messiah, according to the synoptic tradition—and the evangelists too—did not depend on familiarity with the historical facts of his life, but on knowledge of a different kind, the kind that came to expression in the legends of his birth and childhood. It is important to note that this knowledge does not depend on the stories of Jesus' birth and childhood; instead of providing knowledge of historical facts, the infancy narratives are legends drawing from knowledge of a different derivation. The source of this knowledge will remain a concern throughout this investigation; for now we turn our attention to the legends.

B. THE DIVINE GENERATION AND THE MATTHEAN AND LUKAN INFANCY NARRATIVES (LUKE 1:26–38; MATT. 1:18–23; LUKE 2:1–52)

The divine generation stories and the infancy narratives in Matthew and Luke have no parallels; the Gospels of Matthew and Luke tell their own separate stories. The parallel traditions in the Gospels begin only with the preaching of John the Baptist (Mark 1:2–6, //s).

The function of all these stories is to tell who Jesus was. Divine generation stories say that he was born, not of a human father, but of God, and the infancy narratives make the reader aware that he was not an ordinary child. All of these are legends, but legends can be a powerful means of expressing the significance of a person. One can be almost certain that none of the events narrated in these stories actually happened, and yet they are the means by which New Testament Christians educated those to whom these traditions were handed down about who Jesus actually was. If we do not seek historical facts about the life of Jesus in these stories, we will recognize in them important sources for understanding how Jesus was perceived in the communities in which they were developed and handed down.

Two stories narrate what is usually referred to as the virgin birth, Luke 1:26–38 and Matthew 1:18–25. Their primary focus, however, is not the virginity of Mary, but that Jesus was born, not of a human father, but of God, through the Holy Spirit. In the Lukan story the announcement to Mary of the prospective birth of her son is loosely connected to the stories about the birth of John the Baptist (1:5–80). On these follow the stories of the actual birth and the early childhood of Jesus (2:1–52). The Matthean story of the virgin birth is much more closely connected to the rest of Matthew's infancy narratives (2:1–23). We will first discuss the Lukan divine generation story by itself and then the Matthean story along with the infancy narratives. After that we will discuss the Lukan stories about the birth and childhood of Jesus.

1. THE ANNUNCIATION (LUKE 1:26–38; #3)

In its present form the annunciation is the story of the announcement to Mary that she will conceive a child of the Holy Spirit and that the child will be the Davidic messiah, the Son of God. The story has two distinct emphases—the prediction of the Davidic messiahship in the first part (vv. 31–33), and the child's conception through the Holy Spirit in the second (vv. 34–35). In the first part the angel Gabriel announces to Mary that she will conceive and bear a child, apparently from Joseph to whom she was betrothed, and that the child will be the one who will sit on the throne of David—the Davidic messiah, the (adopted) Son of God.

The entire announcement is drawn from Scripture. "You will conceive and bear a child and you will call him Jesus" comes from Isaiah 7:14 (cf. also Gen. 16:11, Judg. 13:3, 5), except that Isaiah writes "Immanuel" and not "Jesus." The passage depends most heavily, however, on 2 Samuel 7:12–14 in which God announces to David through Nathan, the prophet, "And when your days are filled and you are gathered with your fathers, I will raise your seed after you . . . and I will prepare his kingdom. He will build a house in my name, and I will uphold his throne in eternity. I will be a father to him, and he will be a son to me." Nathan's prophecy originally referred to Solomon; in Luke it is taken as a prophecy of the messiah. A number of the key concepts in the angel's announcement to Mary are easily recognizable in the Nathan prophecy, particularly that the child will be called "the son of the most high" ("I will be a father to him, and he will be a son to me"), that "the Lord God will give to him the throne of his father David" ("I will raise your seed after you"), and that "his kingdom will be without end" ("I will uphold his throne in eternity"). Each of these sayings could be understood within the framework of Jewish messianic expectations. The messiah would be the adopted son of God.

The way in which Jews in the time of Jesus understood the messiah as the son of God is shown by the **Targum** on Psalm 7, an Aramaic paraphrase of the Hebrew Scriptures. Translated from the original Hebrew, Psalm 2:7 reads, "You are my son; this day I have given birth to you." In the Targum paraphrase it reads, "You are dear to me as a son to his father; innocent as if I have created you this day." By interpreting the expression in the psalm metaphorically, the Targum paraphrase makes it clear that the person addressed, that is, the messiah, was not the physically generated son of God, but his adopted son, which would agree with the original sense of the psalm. The paraphrase tries to avoid an understanding of the messiah's sonship of God precisely in the sense of Luke's and Matthew's divine generation stories. For Jewish thought, nothing unsettling appears in Luke's story of the annunciation up to verse 33. In a Jewish sense, that the son who was to be born to Mary and Joseph was to have been called "son of the most high" would have been understood in the sense of the Targum paraphrase of Psalm 2:7 as the adopted son of God. A problem for Jewish thought emerges with what then follows.

The conceptual framework of the annunciation story undergoes a radical change in verses 34–37. A clear break in continuity is evident in Mary's reply to the angel's announcement (v. 34). She replies as if the angel had said that she was *already* pregnant, whereas the angel announced, "You *will* conceive and bear a child" (v. 31). One should take Mary's disclaimer that she has had sexual relations with a man, which is the meaning of "I do not know a man" (v. 34), not so much as a reply to what the angel had said, but as preparation for the angel's following clarification—that the child is to be born of the Holy Spirit (v. 35). In the original version of the story the announcement of the angel that she would conceive and give birth to a child (vv. 30–33) was probably followed by Mary's reply in verse 38, "Behold the maid of the Lord. Let it happen to me in accordance with what you said." Mary's reply in verse 34, along with the angel's explanation that the child is to be conceived of the Holy Spirit, is an insertion that breaks the original flow of the story. The angel's explanation, not Mary's embarrassed reply, is the purpose of the insertion. Her reply serves as a transition to the angel's clarification. That is probably why most readers of the passage do not notice that her disclaimer is incongruent with the angel's announcement. Most of the time we do not read texts purely syntactically as the words and sentences move forward, but globally, forwards as well as backwards. Thus it is not surprising that readers typically have not found a problem with Mary's disclaimer. Globally, her disclaimer makes good sense from the point of view of the angel's clarification.

The insertion of the divine generation into the story should not be interpreted as the arbitrary introduction of an alien idea into the story. When the original Jewish-Christian annunciation story was told to Gentile Christians they took it for granted that the angel, when announcing that the child would be called "the son of the most high" (v. 32), meant that the child would be born of God, that is, would be divinely generated. Many such stories of divine generation were told in Hellenistic antiquity, for example, that of Plato (cf. Diogenes Laertius, *Lives of Great Philosophers* 3.1–2), of Alexander the Great (Plutarch, *Parallel Lives: Alexander* 2.1–3.2), and of Augustus Caesar (Suetonius, *Lives of the Caesars* 2.9.4). The Lukan insertion merely made explicit what had already been implicit for Gentile ears when they heard the Jewish-Christian story. For such Gentile ears the original emphasis on the Davidic messiahship of the child was of little significance because a Davidic messiah had little if any meaning in a non-Jewish environment.

It is not clear whether Luke himself was responsible for the insertion concerning the divine generation or whether he already found it in his source. He was, however, almost certainly responsible for the introduction of verses 36–37, "Look, Elizabeth your relative is also pregnant with a child, even though she is already old; it is for her who is called sterile already the sixth month; for nothing is impossible for God." With the reference to Elizabeth's pregnancy Luke connected this and other stories of the birth of Jesus with those concerning John the Baptist. By means of such interconnections Luke established the relationship between Jesus and John in a way that made it clear that Jesus was the more important figure. John no longer had an independent meaning; his meaning was derived from his relationship to Jesus. This was not originally true. We will return to the relationship between John and Jesus below in chapter 2 on John the Baptist and Jesus.

The story of the annunciation in the original Jewish Christian version (vv. 26–33, 38) shows that a Davidic messiahship of Jesus could have been completely at home in certain early Christian traditions. At the same time, in its present form the story shows how easily such a tradition was adapted to express a Gentile Christian conception—by shifting the emphasis from Jesus' Davidic lineage to his divine sonship through the Holy Spirit. As we will see below, the question of Jesus' sonship of David was addressed more directly in Mark 12:35–37a, //s. It is an issue we will also encounter in connection with the genealogies of Jesus (Matt. 1:2–17; Luke 3:23–38).

2. THE MATTHEAN BIRTH STORIES (MATT. 1:18–2:23; #7–8, 10–11)

The birth narrative in Matthew 1:18–2:23 is composed of two originally separate narratives, a cycle of Joseph stories (1:18–25; 2:13–15, 19–23), and the story of the magi and Herod (2:1–12, 16–18). They are bound together by Matthew in a single narrative concerning the birth and infancy of Jesus.

The quotations from Scripture in these stories were almost certainly introduced by Matthew. Other examples of this kind of quotation in the Gospel are introduced with variants of the formula, "This happened in order to fulfill the word spoken by the Lord through the prophet, saying, . . ." The following quotations appear to have been introduced into the stories by Matthew: 1:22–23; 2:6, 15b, 17–18. A formula referring to a word spoken by a prophet without an actual quotation appears in 2:23b.

The following display of the text of Matthew 1:18–2:23 highlights its structural features. For that reason the translation is very literal at places in order to bring out the parallel formulations. The formula quotations are indented. Joseph stories are preceded by Roman numerals, while the paragraphs in the magi and Herod story are lettered A and B. Italics identify words and phrases that are repeated.

The Text of Matthew 1:18–2:23

1:18 The birth of Jesus was like this:
When his mother Mary was betrothed to Joseph, before they had come together, it was found that she was pregnant of the Holy Spirit. ¹⁹So Joseph, her husband, being just, but not wanting to expose her, planned to send her away quietly.

I. ²⁰*When he was deliberating these things, behold, an angel of the Lord appeared to him in a dream, saying,*

Joseph, son of David, do not be afraid to *take your wife* Mary, for what is conceived in her is from the Holy Spirit;

²¹She will give birth to a son, and *you will call him Jesus, for* he will save his people from their sins.

²²All of this happened in order to fulfill the word spoken by the Lord through the prophet saying,²³ Behold a young woman will conceive and bear a son. And they will call him Emmanuel, which is translated, God with us.

²⁴And after Joseph rose from the dream he did as the angel of the Lord commanded him,

²⁵and *he took his wife*, and he did not "know" her until she gave birth to a son, and he *called him Jesus*.

A. ²:¹*When Jesus was born* in Bethlehem in Judea in the days of Herod the king, behold, magi from the east came to Jerusalem, ²saying, Where is the newborn king of the Jews? For we have seen his star in the east, and we came to worship him.

B. ³*When king Herod heard*, he was disturbed, and all of Jerusalem with him; ⁴and calling together the chief priests and scribes of the people he asked them where the messiah was to be born, ⁵and they said, in Bethlehem in Judea,

⁶For thus it is written by the prophet: And you Bethlehem, land of Judah, will in no way be the least among the tribes of Judah, for from you will proceed a leader who will shepherd my people Israel.

B. ⁷*Then Herod, when he called* the magi together secretly, inquired from them the time when the star appeared, ⁸and sending them to Bethlehem he said, Go and inquire exactly concerning the child; when you have found him, let me know, so that I too can come and worship him.

A. ⁹*When they heard* the king they went away; and behold the star which they saw in the east went before them until it came and stayed above the place where the child was.

A. ¹⁰*When they saw* the star they rejoiced with a great joy; ¹¹and when they arrived at the house they saw the child with Mary, his mother, and falling on their knees they worshiped him; and opening their treasures they gave him gifts, gold and frankincense and myrrh. ¹²But when they received an oracle in a dream not to return to Herod they went to their country by another way.

II. ¹³*When they left, behold, an angel of the Lord appeared to Joseph in a dream, saying,*
After you have risen, take the child and his mother and flee *to Egypt, and* remain *there until* I tell you, *for* Herod will seek the boy to kill him.

¹⁴*And after he rose he took the child and his mother* at night, *and* he went *to Egypt,* ¹⁵ and he was *there until* the death of Herod;

in order to fulfill the word of the Lord spoken by the prophet saying, From Egypt I will call my son.

B. [16]*Then Herod, when he saw* that he was deceived by the magi, became very angry, and he sent to have killed all the boys in Bethlehem and in all its environs from two years down, in accordance with the time he learned from the magi.

> [17]Then was fulfilled what was spoken by the prophet, saying, [18]A voice was heard in Rama, wailing and a great lament, Rachel mourning her children, and she did not want to be consoled, because they were no longer.

III. [19]*When Herod died, behold, an angel of the Lord appeared to Joseph in a dream* in Egypt, [20]*saying,*
After you have risen, take the child and his mother and go to the land of Israel, for those who seek the life of the child have died.
And [21]*after he rose he took the child and his mother and* went *into the land of Israel.*

[22]But when he heard the Archelaus reigned over Judea in the place of his father, Herod, he was afraid to go there, and being warned in a dream he withdrew to the district of Galilee, [23]and went and dwelt in a city called Nazareth,

> that what was spoken by the prophet might be fulfilled, that he will be called a Nazarene.

Taking note of the Joseph stories first, we find that, with the exception of the last one (2:22–23), they all have the same form.

1. All of them begin with a phrase that refers back to what had happened just previously (in the Greek it is a genitive absolute construction): "But as he considered this . . ." (1:20), "now, when they had departed . . ." (2:13), and "but when Herod died . . ." (2:19).
2. This is followed in each case by the statement "behold, an angel of the Lord appeared to him in a dream, saying . . ." (1:20; 2:13, 19).
3. The angel gives Joseph instructions, a double set in the first story (cf. vv. 20 and 21, respectively), and one set each in the second and third stories (2:13 and 20). In the latter two stories the instructions are introduced with "when you have risen" (the RSV has "Rise"), which, as we will see below, also holds formal significance.
4. For each set of instructions the angel gives a reason, introduced with "for" (1:20–21; 2:13, 20).
5. It is then reported in almost the same words spoken by the angel that Joseph carried out the instructions of the angel (1:25; 2:14, 21). This is a structural feature expressing that Joseph "did [exactly] as the angel of the Lord commanded him" (1:24).
6. The narration of Joseph carrying out the angel's instructions is prefaced in each case with "after he rose" (1:24; 2:14, 21), echoing the "after

you have risen" of the angel's instructions in 2:13 and 20. The identical Greek word is used in all these cases. The RSV translates more freely.

The final Joseph story (2:22–23) contains structural features similar to these—Joseph also receives instructions in a dream—but it is clear that in terms of formal structure it is at best an imitation. Furthermore, it appears to be an appendage; after it had already been stated that Joseph entered the land of Israel it must have occurred to someone (Matthew himself?) that Joseph could not return to Bethlehem but must instead go to Nazareth because that is where Jesus was to grow up. That Matthew himself may have been responsible for the formulation of these verses is shown by their structural similarity to 4:12–14, which, as we will see later, may have had great relevance for the way in which Matthew composed his Gospel.

Matthew 2:22–23	Matthew 4:12–14 (#30, 32)
But when he heard that Archelaus reigned over Judea in place of his father, Herod, he was afraid to go there, and being warned in a dream, *he withdrew into* the district of *Galilee,* *and he went and dwelt* in a city called Nazareth,	*But* [the RSV has "now"] *when he heard* that John had been arrested *he withdrew into Galilee,* *and,* leaving Nazareth, *he went and dwelt* in Capernaum by the Sea, in the territory of Zebulun and Naphtali,
that what was spoken by the prophet might be fulfilled . . .	*that what was spoken by the* prophet Isaiah *might be fulfilled . . .*

A clear connection between these two passages is also suggested by the fact that in the first it is stated that Jesus (with his family) moved to Nazareth (2:23), and in the second passage that he left Nazareth and moved to Capernaum (4:13). This will concern us again later, after we have discussed the genealogies.

In Matthew 1:20–25, 2:13–15, and 2:20–21, thus, we have a cycle of three stories about Joseph, the father of Jesus, who receives instructions from an angel in dreams, which he carries out exactly as commanded. The formal similarity in the structure of these stories leaves little doubt that they originally belonged together. The cycle was probably introduced by 1:18–19, "The birth of Jesus was like this: When his mother Mary was betrothed to Joseph . . ." although Matthew may have reformulated verse 18a in order to connect the entire passage, that is, 1:18–2:23, with the beginning of the Gospel. In Greek the word for "genealogy" (1:1) and "birth" (1:18) is the same. In addition to editorial changes, Matthew also introduced into these stories the two formula quotations (1:22–23 and

2:15). He was probably also responsible for the formulation of 2:22–23, which he structured to conform partly, but not completely, to the existing cycle of Joseph stories.

The remaining part of this section in Matthew contains the story of the magi (2:1–12) and of Herod's murder of the children of Bethlehem and environs (2:16–18). The story of the magi has five clearly marked paragraphs, each beginning in the RSV with "when" (2:1, 3, 9, and 10), and in one case "then" (v. 7). In the Greek they are marked by a participle, which would require that verse 7 also have a "when" if it is translated literally: "Then Herod, when he . . ." as in verse 16. The Greek reads exactly the same in both cases. The additional "then" in verse 7 (compared with the beginnings of the other paragraphs) serves to mark more sharply the transition from verses 1–6 to verses 7–12, that is, from the first two paragraphs to the last three.

In each of the paragraphs the role of the main actor(s) is fulfilled by either the magi or Herod, as follows: magi (vv. 1–2), Herod (vv. 3–5), again Herod (vv. 7–8), magi (v. 9), and again the magi (vv. 10–11). This gives the following schema: ABBAA. However, if we consider the sharper transition between the second and third paragraphs it may look like this: AB BAA. The final A leaves the schema unbalanced, but that could be intentional, the imbalance weighing in favor of the final paragraph when the magi arrive and worship the newborn Jesus.

However, if we consider that the story of Herod's murder of the children (2:16) begins in the same way as the third paragraph (v. 7), and that "when he saw that he had been tricked by the magi" links this remaining story up with that of the magi, the conclusion is almost unavoidable: Herod's murder of the children is the last scene in what now appears to be a story contrasting the magi and Herod. The culmination of the story reveals the true character of each; the magi find the child and worship him, whereas Herod tries to destroy him in an act of harsh brutality. The transition to the final story is again sharper, "*Then* Herod, *when* he saw that he had been tricked" (2:16), similar to 2:7, "*Then* Herod, *when* he called the magi together secretly, inquired from them the time when the star appeared."

The story may also reflect a tension between Jerusalem and Bethlehem, indicated by the more sharply marked transition in verse 7 from the first two "Jerusalem" and the last four "Bethlehem" paragraphs. That Jerusalem belongs with Herod is confirmed by the fact that the magi's announcement in verse 2 disturbs not only Herod, but "all Jerusalem with him" (v. 3). Jerusalem appears to have shared Herod's dislike for the child who had been born.

That the story of the magi and Herod may have had more than one step in its composition is indicated by the different ways in which the star is understood in verses 2 and 9. In verse 1 it is an astrological sign that the magi observe in the east and interpret to mean that a royal child has been born for the Jews. That is why they go to Jerusalem, the obvious place to seek a newborn Jewish prince. In verse 9, however, it is not an astrological sign but a star that leads them to the child. It is incomprehensible why in such a case the magi had to go to Jerusalem first and why Herod had to inform them that they would find the infant in Bethlehem. It would be futile to try to unravel these early stages in the composition of the story; we do not have sufficient information on which to base such an unraveling.

In the composition of his birth narratives Matthew thus appears to have combined a cycle of Joseph stories with a story of the magi and Herod, integrating them skillfully into what is now a series of stories concerning the birth of Jesus. Whereas Joseph, on the one hand, and the magi and Herod, on the other, were the central figures in the original stories, only Jesus could function as such once the stories were combined; Jesus is the only one who plays a part in all of them. In this way Jesus' birth, which was only the occasion for the original stories, became their central theme. Matthew's shift in emphasis is reinforced by the formula quotations, which can be seen most clearly in the quotation of 2:15: the original focus was on Joseph's obedient actions (2:13–15a); the formula quotation shifts the focus to God calling his son from Egypt (v. 15bc) and so from Joseph as the central figure to Jesus.

Matthew undoubtedly made editorial changes when he combined the stories, for example, by beginning the second Joseph story with "after they [the magi] left" (2:13) in order to connect it to the story of the magi and Herod. In the case of verse 16 Matthew maintained the original reference to the present verse 12, skipping the second Joseph story. He had no choice in the sequence of the stories since the flight to Egypt had to come after the visit of the magi and before the murder of the children. In addition, as already indicated, Matthew was almost certainly responsible for the formula quotations (1:22–23; 2:6, 15b, and 17–18), for the story of the move to Nazareth (2:22–23), and for the formulation of the present introduction (1:18a) with which he related these stories to the beginning of the Gospel and the genealogy of Jesus (1:1).

3. THE LUKAN BIRTH AND CHILDHOOD STORIES (LUKE 2:1–52; #7–9, 11–12)

As we have seen, the Matthean birth narratives were originally a cycle of stories about Joseph, the pious father of Jesus, and a single story about the magi and Herod, narrating their involvement in incidents related to the birth of Jesus. As the one person who was involved in all of them, Jesus became the central focus of these stories when they were combined in Matthew's Gospel. In the Lukan birth and childhood stories Jesus was the central focus from the beginning and would be so even if one took the stories individually. This is true also of Luke's story of the annunciation (1:26–38), which we discussed earlier. It is interesting to note, however, that in the context of the stories of the birth of John the Baptist in which

Luke placed the annunciation, the focus is broadened to include also John the Baptist. Luke evidently did this intentionally, for example, when he made the angel draw Mary's attention to the fact that John's mother, Elizabeth, was already pregnant (1:36–37).

According to the Matthean birth stories Jesus was born in Bethlehem, his parents' hometown, before it became necessary for them to flee to Egypt. When they returned to Israel, however, they did not return to Bethlehem because they feared Archelaus; they moved to Nazareth instead (Matt. 2:22–23). These moves made it possible to reconcile the assumption that, as the messiah, Jesus must have been born in Bethlehem (Mic. 5:1–3, cf. Matt. 2:6) with the knowledge that he grew up in Nazareth. Luke resolves the conflict between Bethlehem and Nazareth in a different way. According to him Joseph and Mary were already residing in Nazareth before the birth of Jesus, but the requirements of a census brought them to Bethlehem where the child was born (2:1–7).

It is worth noting that it was not always assumed that Jesus was born of Davidic descent in Bethlehem. According to John 7:40–43, some people suggested that Jesus was indeed the prophet, but when others suggested that he was the messiah, they responded by asking, "Is the messiah then to come from Galilee? Does Scripture not say that the messiah comes from the seed of David, and from Bethlehem, the village of David?" The assumption is clearly that Jesus came from Galilee, not from Bethlehem, and that he was not of Davidic descent. The Matthean and Lukan birth stories were probably produced precisely to lay to rest such questions. We will return to John 7:40–43 below in the section on the question concerning the messiah as son of David.

Luke could have been responsible for some of the details of his story of the birth of Jesus, for example, the dating of the event (v. 2). He also dates the beginning of the activity of John the Baptist in 3:1–2, probably as a way of locating the history of salvation in world history in accord with his remark in Acts 26:26, "These events did not take place in a corner." He was probably also responsible for mentioning the emperor Augustus in verse 1—Roman emperors are mentioned by name in the New Testament only by Luke (also in Acts 11:28 and 18:2)—and possibly for identifying the census as the occasion for the journey to Bethlehem.

The conclusion, "and she wrapped him in swaddling clothes and laid him in a manger because there was no place for them in the inn" (v. 7), is no longer part of the story of the birth but forms a transition to the story of the shepherds (vv. 8–20). One should not make a big issue of the fact that there had been no place for Joseph and Mary in the inn. That statement is included to explain why the child was placed in a manger, which in turn is more a feature of the story of the shepherds who found the child in a manger (v. 16) than of the birth story itself. In antiquity the foundling child who turned out to be a prince was frequently found by a shepherd, the most renowned being Oedipus. Also worth mentioning here is that if Jesus was the son of a carpenter (cf. Matt. 13:55), better translated "cabinetmaker," he was hardly the poor child he is frequently presented to have been. If Joseph was actually a carpenter the family probably belonged rather comfortably to what might be called the middle class of Nazareth, that is, he does not appear to have belonged to the privileged few of the upper classes in Palestine, but neither does he seem to have been part of the deprived multitudes of peasants and day laborers.

In the second story (vv. 8–20) shepherds in the fields at night are surprised by the appearance of an angel who tells them that "the savior, who is the Lord messiah, was born today in the city of David" (v. 11). As a sign of legitimation the angel tells them that they will find an infant "wrapped in swaddling clothes, lying in a manger" (v. 12). After the angels leave, the shepherds say to each other, "Let us go to Bethlehem and see this thing which the Lord has revealed to us" (v. 15). It should be noted that they "go to" Bethlehem and thus were not necessarily in its close vicinity. After they find Jesus and his parents they recognize the sign of legitimation that had been given to them by the angel (v. 17).

Luke probably did not leave the story unedited. He may have been responsible for the comment that "Mary held on to these things, thinking them over in her heart" (v. 19), which is repeated in the story of the twelve-year-old Jesus in Jerusalem (v. 51). It has been suggested that there is a contradiction between verses 18 and 20. According to verse 18, "everyone who heard the shepherds" was amazed, but this happens even before they had left the scene where they found the child to tell others about it (cf. v. 20). However, "everyone" could refer to those present at the stable, particularly Joseph and Mary, who were equally surprised at the blessing that Simeon pronounced over the child in the next story (v. 33). It is even possible that both comments (vv. 18 and 33) were editorial insertions by means of which Luke provided continuity between the stories.

The sudden appearance of the heavenly host (vv. 13–14) may be an addition, not necessarily by Luke, although "glory to God in the highest, and peace on earth" (v. 14), is reminiscent of the specifically Lukan words spoken at Jesus' entry into Jerusalem, "peace in heaven, and glory in the highest" (19:38).

Luke's story of Jesus' birth has the appearance of a Davidic messianic legend; it probably originated in Jewish Christian circles. Luke undoubtedly understood it in a much broader sense of Jesus as "the savior who is Christ the Lord" (v. 11), who was proclaimed "in all of Judea and Samaria and to the ends of the earth" (Acts 1:8). This more universal view comes to expression already in the blessing of Simeon, "My eyes have seen your salvation which you have prepared before the eyes of all the nations" (v. 30, quoted from Isa. 52:10).

Luke himself may have been responsible for the next brief statement concerning the circumcision of Jesus (v. 21). It appears to be based on a detail from his story of the annunciation that the child should be called Jesus (cf. 1:31). Although it has the appearance of a separate story, Luke probably intended it to be seen in close connection with the story of the so-called presentation of Jesus in the temple (vv. 22–38). Taken together, these two stories formally resemble the story of the birth and circumcision of John (1:57–80), which we will discuss below. It is noteworthy that the birth and circumcision of John is also coordinated with the announcement of his birth (1:5–25). In the story of John's birth special attention is also given to the name that was to be given the expected child (v. 13, cf. 1:59–63), and his birth story too is concluded with prophetic announcements (1:67–79).

The formal resemblance between the stories of the announcement and birth of John and of Jesus may provide an answer to individual problems that have been encountered in connection with the prophetic pronouncements of each of these stories. In the case of the so-called Benedictus of Zechariah, it had been observed that the first part (1:68–75) is very general and could have been relevant for any messianic child, whereas the second part concerns specifically John (1:76–79). In the case of Simeon too there are two separate blessings, a general one that could have been relevant for any messianic child (2:29–32), and a second, addressed to Mary, which concerns specifically Jesus, including a parenthetical statement about Mary herself (2:34–35). The two successive blessings of Simeon thus appear to have a model in the dual benediction of Zachariah, revealing at the same time that the Benedictus could have been formulated intentionally in that way. Since Luke was obviously aware of the dual nature of the blessings and did not experience it as a problem, neither should we.

The connection of the statement concerning the circumcision and naming of Jesus and the story of Simeon's blessing is by association only; the two stories as such remain compositionally separate, revealing the secondary nature of the connection.

The reasons given for the parents' visit to the temple with the child Jesus are probably secondary. Leviticus 12:6 and 8, quoted respectively in verses 22 and 24, require only the presence of the mother in the temple. That may be why Exodus 13:2 is also quoted (v. 23), although it too does not require that the child be brought to the temple. The original story probably mentioned only Simeon's blessing of Jesus when the infant was brought to the temple without giving a reason why he was taken there. It is possible that in the earliest versions of the story the blessing did not take place in the temple. The central theme is the prophetic blessing of the child by the saintly old man, similar to Zechariah's blessing of John. There is a remarkably similar legend of the aged ascetic Asita who came to the palace of the Buddha's father by divine inspiration and, taking the newborn child in his arms, prophesied the great future that the child would have, but that he no longer expected to see. Dependence of the Lukan story on the Buddhist legend is not indicated by this similarity.

The story of Anna the prophetess (vv. 36–38) is attached secondarily to the story of Simeon's blessing, duplicating it in many ways, except that an actual blessing is not included. Noteworthy is that she witnesses to those "who expect the redemption of Jerusalem" (v. 38), indicating Davidic messianic expectations in the Jesus tradition.

Since Joseph and Mary already lived in Nazareth, Luke states that they returned there and that Jesus grew up in that village (vv. 39–40). But Luke has it that the parents went regularly to Jerusalem for the Passover (v. 41), and he adds the story of their taking the twelve-year-old Jesus along (vv. 42–52). On their way home they discover they have lost him (vv. 44–45), and they find him three days later in the temple, discussing with the teachers who are amazed at his wisdom (vv. 46–47). Similar stories of the youthful wisdom of other great religious figures appear in antiquity, for example, that of Moses (Philo, *Life of Moses* 1.21, and Josephus, *Antiquities* 2.9:6). Josephus even boasts about his own wisdom at an early age, similar to that of Jesus here (*Life* 9).

Mary expresses her anxiety to Jesus, telling him how worried she and "your" father have been (v. 49), but Jesus counters that he is indeed busy with the things of "my father" (v. 50), revealing Mary's ignorance of Jesus' real, that is, not merely physical, father. The exchange between them makes it obvious that divine generation is not presupposed in the story. The repeated amazement of Jesus' parents each time they learn something new about the child (cf. vv. 18, 33) would be surprising if the annunciation is presupposed, even if it did not include the part on the divine generation. For example, nothing in the blessing of Simeon (vv. 29–32), except its more universalist tone, supersedes what the angel announced to Mary (1:30–33). Nothing in what Simeon said should have caused Mary or Joseph to be amazed (cf. 2:33). We may conclude that the birth and childhood stories in Luke were originally independent of the story of the annunciation and probably also relatively independent of each other.

Conclusion. Aside from the fact that he grew up in Nazareth, the birth and childhood stories of Jesus do not provide historical information. And yet, these legends may be more revealing about him than stories that are primarily concerned with historical facts. The story of his reception in Nazareth reveals that historically establishable facts could stand in the way of understanding Jesus' real meaning. The legends of his birth and infancy do not provide historical data about Jesus but rather express who he was; what is conveyed in all of the Gospels is that Jesus was more than what could be perceived historically. The legends, including the stories of divine intervention in connection with his birth, are tools used by New Testament Christians to express their perception of Jesus. Their understanding of him was probably more accurate than that of the Nazarenes, who relied on purely factual evidence.

Knowing this still does not answer the question of how Jesus' followers came to hold such an understanding of him. It is a question that will continue to occupy our minds as we proceed with our investigation. For now we turn to a passage dealing specifically with the messiahship of Jesus and with the problem of his origins in Nazareth, which contradicted the understanding that the messiah was supposed to have been born in Bethlehem. As we have seen, the Matthean and Lukan birth stories, each in its own way, tried to establish a birth in Bethlehem for Jesus, notwithstanding his origin in Nazareth. As the next passage shows, the followers of Jesus did not always try to reconcile his growing up in Nazareth with a birth in Bethlehem.

C. THE QUESTION CONCERNING THE SONSHIP OF DAVID (MARK 12:35–37a, //s; #283; cf. JOHN 7:40–43)

Many passages in the New Testament show that regarding Jesus as a descendant of David was a favorite way of expressing his messiahship. For example, Luke states, "The Lord God will give him the throne of his father David" (Luke 1:32); the crowds at his entry into Jerusalem hail him with "hosanna to the son of David" (Matt. 21:9); and the blind Bartimaeus calls to him for help, "Have mercy on me, son of David" (Mark 10:47–48, //s). However, this idea alone was not always considered adequate. So, for example, Paul quotes a tradition in Romans 1:3b–4 that moves beyond the sonship of David to the sonship of God: "Who was born of the seed of David *in the flesh*, [but] pronounced the Son of God in power *through the Holy Spirit* at [his] resurrection from the dead." According to the tradition quoted by Paul, Jesus had been a descendant of David, but his true significance went beyond that: his sonship of David through his birth was a matter of the flesh; it was through the Holy Spirit, at his resurrection from the dead that he was pronounced, that is, became, the Son of God.

Our present passage may have been understood in a similar way by Mark and the other synoptic evangelists, not with regard to the way in which they understood Jesus to have been the Son of God, but in the sense that even as the son of David, he was David's Lord. All three evangelists quote sayings in which Jesus is addressed as the son of David (for example, Mark 10:47, //s; #264), revealing that they did not doubt that he had been a descendant of David; for them he must have been understood to have been both a son of David and more than a son of David. As we will see, a similar concept may be expressed in Matthew's genealogy (Matt. 1:2–17; #6), according to which Jesus was a descendant of David through Joseph (1:1), but because he was not the physical son of Joseph (cf. 1:16), he was more than a son of David: he was the son of God. Something similar may be involved in Luke's genealogy (Luke 2:23–38; #19). All three synoptic evangelists probably understood the present passage in more or less the same way. For them the point of the psalm was not to deny that Jesus was the son of David, but to emphasize that he was more than David's son: he was David's Lord.

The idea of Jesus as superior to David, however, was probably not the original meaning of the present passage. Taken by itself, the passage questions the identification of the messiah with the son of David: "David himself calls him Lord; how then is he his son?" Clear proof that not everyone assumed that Jesus was of Davidic descent can be found in John 7:40–53 (#241): "How would the messiah come from Galilee? Does Scripture not say that the messiah comes from the seed of David, and from Bethlehem, the village of David?" (vv. 41–42). The understanding in John is plainly that Jesus came from Galilee, not Bethlehem, and that he was not a descendant of David; thus he could not have been the messiah. The fourth evangelist gives no evidence of disputing the statement that Jesus had not been born in Bethlehem as a descendant of David. He himself may not have believed it either, but for him the messiahship of Jesus was not to be understood in those categories. His view was probably similar to the original intent of the passage, which can be perceived as an exact answer to the question raised in John 7:41–42: how could Jesus be the son of David if David himself calls him his Lord? David's own pronouncement affirmed that the messiah was not to have been his son.

The three versions of the story in the synoptics are so different that we are unable to determine whether or not Matthew and Luke quoted from Mark. The only significant verbal agreement among the three evangelists is in the quotation from Scripture, but even then Luke reads "a stool for your feet"(v. 43) against Mark and Matthew's "under your feet" (Mark 12:36; Matt. 22:44). Matthew adds a concluding statement (v. 46), but it has little significance as far as the passage itself is concerned. The changes in Matthew and Luke could have been made by the evangelists themselves, but it is equally possible that each of them quoted the tradition differently as they remembered it. If that were the case, it must have been a well-established tradition, because the three versions contain such similar material, notwithstanding the differences in verbal formulation.

Conclusion. It thus appears that not all the followers of Jesus solved the problem posed by his childhood in Nazareth by claiming that he had nevertheless been born in Bethlehem. Our passage disclaims any significance of the Davidic messiahship for the meaning of Christ, a view that appears to have been shared by the fourth evangelist. As we will see, the conception of a Davidic messiahship was indeed too confining to express fully the meaning of Jesus, not only, but especially when, Christianity spread beyond the borders of Palestine. Nevertheless, the more typical view of Jesus' earliest followers was that represented by the legends of his birth in Bethlehem. Those legends as such, however, did not answer the question concerning his sonship of David. It is a question with which Matthew and Luke dealt by means of their genealogies of Jesus. Both maintained that Jesus had indeed been a descendant of David and yet more than a descendant of David by claiming Joseph for his father, but not in a physical sense.

D. THE GENEALOGIES (MATT. 1:1–17; #6; LUKE 3:23–38; #19)

The genealogies in Matthew and in Luke differ from each other in a number of ways: Matthew goes back only to Abraham, Luke all the way to Adam and to God; Matthew begins with Abraham and comes down to Jesus, whereas Luke begins with Jesus and works back to God; and Matthew places his genealogy at the beginning of his Gospel, whereas Luke's follows the baptism of Jesus. There are also internal differences in the actual lists of names.

The Matthean genealogy is based on 1 Chronicles 2:1–15 (cf. Ruth 4:12–22) for the list from Jacob to David (vv. 2–6), and on 1 Chronicles 3:5–19 for the list from David to Zerubbabel (vv. 7–12). From there it proceeds on its own down to Joseph and Jesus, disregarding the rest of the names in 1 Chronicles 3:19–24. We do not know from where Matthew gets these names in his genealogy.

For the extension of the list back from Abraham to Adam the Lukan genealogy (vv. 34–38) follows 1 Chronicles 1:1–34 (cf. Gen. 5:1–27; 11:10–26). Luke agrees with Matthew in following 1 Chronicles 2:1–15 (Ruth 4:12–22) from Jacob to David (vv. 31–34), but in the reverse order, and he has Admin instead of Aram in verse 25. From there, however, his genealogy follows a lineage from David over Nathan to Ner (vv. 27–31), not over Solomon as in Matthew and in 1 Chronicles 3, but then he agrees with them again with Salathiel and Zerubbabel (v. 27). From there Luke again goes his own way down to Joseph (vv. 23–27). We also do not know from where Luke gets the names that do not occur in 1 Chronicles. We do know that both genealogies were taken from the Greek text of Chronicles, because they both have Salathiel as the father of Zerubbabel in agreement with the **Septuagint** (Matt. 1:12; Luke 3:27), whereas the Hebrew has Pedaiah.

Matthew's genealogy is arranged in three sets of fourteen names each, as he himself states in verse 17, fourteen generations from Abraham to David (of David), fourteen from David to the Babylonian exile (vv. 6–11), and fourteen from the exile to Christ (vv. 11–16), but the third set has only thirteen names. No satisfactory solution for the missing name in the third set has been found. This should not be a matter of great concern since it does not materially affect anything. The inclusion of four women in the list, Tamar (v. 3), Rahab, Ruth (v. 5), and Bathsheba, the wife of Uriah (v. 6), does not call for a special explanation since two of the names already occur in 1 Chronicles, that is, Tamar (2:4, cf. Ruth 4:12) and Bathsheba (3:5).

Significant about the Matthean genealogy is that it traces the lineage of Jesus back beyond David to Abraham. The concern apparently was not merely to establish Jesus' sonship of David; by reaching back through the generations to Abraham the genealogy evidently links Jesus with the entire history of Israel. The symmetry of the three sets each of fourteen generations rounds off the history of Israel, which begins with Abraham and ends with Jesus. By moving beyond David to Abraham the genealogy may already suggest that "more than David" is involved (cf. Mark 12:35–37, //s).

This "more than David" is clearly indicated by the present form of the genealogy, which avoids taking Joseph as the father of Jesus: "Joseph, the husband of Mary, out of whom Jesus, who is called Christ, was born" (v. 16). Jesus is thus the culmination of the three sets of fourteen generations representing Israel and yet is not one of them. As the Son of God through the Holy Spirit he is more than just another member of the list of generations. And yet the connection through Joseph remains important in Matthew because it is to him that the angel says, "Joseph, son of David, do not fear to take your wife, for that which was conceived in her is from the Holy Spirit" (v. 20).

It is possible that the original genealogy did interpret Joseph as the father of Jesus, that is, that it had been formulated before the understanding of Jesus as the divinely generated son of God had been developed. The genealogy makes sense only if Jesus was the son of Joseph, not if his birth bypassed Joseph. The involvement of Joseph continued to cause problems in the tradition of Matthew's text. That is, it remained in conflict with the understanding that Jesus was not Joseph's, but God's son; a number of manuscripts refer to Joseph as the "betrothed" rather than the "husband" of Mary. Matthew connected his genealogy with the divine generation story (1:18–25) and the other infancy narratives (2:1–23) by means of the Greek catchword *genesis*, which means "birth" in 1:18, "descent" in 1:1.

Luke states plainly that Jesus was only supposed to have been the son of Joseph (v. 23). Such an understanding defeats the purpose of the genealogy since the latter obviously wants to trace Jesus' descent from God through all the generations, including Joseph. In that way it could be understood as an alternate explanation of Jesus' sonship of God, in contrast to both the divine generation (1:35–36) and the pronouncement of him as the Son of God at his baptism(3:22). The phrase "as was supposed," which is parenthetic, may have been interpolated. If the original intention of the genealogy had been to present Jesus as the son of God, it would remain unconvincing, because in that sense of the sonship of God everyone would be a son or daughter of God. It is unclear what Luke intended by including it. Evidently, the genealogy is somehow connected with the pronouncement of the voice from heaven at the baptism of Jesus on which it follows: "You are my son; the beloved one with whom I am well pleased" (3:22), but its purpose still remains unclear.

Conclusion. The genealogies and the birth and infancy narratives of Jesus interpret his meaning by referring to his origin. The tradition of the question concerning his sonship of David in Mark 12:35–37a and the fact that the fourth evangelist did not consider providing contrary evidence (John 7:40–41) reveal that the issue of sonship had not been settled in early Christianity. The tradition quoted by Paul in Romans 1:3b–4 shows that Jesus' origin as such was not sufficient to determine his meaning. As we have seen, even for Matthew and Luke, being the son of David did not determine who Jesus was. He was the Son of God in a sense that went beyond a Davidic messiahship. What that means begins to become clear in the tradition of the baptism and temptation of Jesus.

E. THE BAPTISM AND TEMPTATION OF JESUS (MARK 1:9–11, 1:12–13, //s)

The stories of Jesus' baptism and temptation mark the move from the activity of John the Baptist (#13–17) to the life and ministry of Jesus. We will return to John and his significance for understanding Jesus in chapter 2 on John the Baptist and Jesus.

1. THE BAPTISM (MARK 1:9–11, //s; #18)

In the Markan story of Jesus' baptism John is still mentioned, but the focus now shifts completely to Jesus. It is Jesus who goes out from Nazareth to be baptized by John: "And it happened in those days that Jesus came from Nazareth of Galilee, and he was baptized in the Jordan by John" (v. 9). It is Jesus who sees the heavens open and the dove descending on him: "And immediately as he came up from the water he saw the heavens split open and the Spirit like a dove descending on him" (v. 10). Anybody else who may have been present, including John, is of no significance whatsoever. It is the moment of illumination for Jesus, in which he is prepared for his ministry by the Holy Spirit descending upon him and the voice from heaven assuring him that he has become the Son of God.

One can recognize the specific meaning of Mark's story by comparing it with the other synoptics. Matthew and Luke describe the onlooker's view of what happened on this important occasion, while Mark focuses on what Jesus experienced. Matthew focuses the reader's attention on the incident: "Behold, the heavens opened, and he saw the spirit of God descending as a dove upon him" (Matt. 3:16). And while Matthew still mentions Jesus seeing the descent of the Spirit as a dove, in Luke the act of seeing (*eiden* in the Greek of Mark and Matthew) is no longer mentioned; the act of seeing has been replaced by referring to the bodily appearance (*eidei*) of the Spirit as a dove: "The heavens opened and the Holy Spirit descended in bodily appearance as a dove upon him" (Luke 3:22). By contrast, Mark does not describe what happened for all to see at the baptism of Jesus; he portrays the event instead as Jesus' experience of illumination.

In the single, majestic event of Jesus' baptism, concisely narrated, Mark expresses what Matthew and Luke used extensive divine generation and infancy narratives to express. Other early Christian traditions understood Jesus to have been made the Son of God at his resurrection. For example, in the tradition quoted by Paul in Romans 1:3b–4, contrary to the divine generation stories, the birth of Jesus was something purely physical, a matter of the flesh; the Spirit became active only at his resurrection: "Who was born of the seed of David in the flesh, but was set apart as the Son of God in power through the Holy Spirit at [his] resurrection from the dead." Similarly in Acts 3:36, "God has made this Jesus whom you have crucified Lord and messiah." The most important of all for understanding the significance of the present story in Mark is the description of Jesus' transfiguration, which in its original form narrated his enthronement as the Son of God after his resurrection (Mark 9:2–10, #161) in the same sense as Peter's statement in Acts 3:36. We will return to the story of the transfiguration below at the end of part 1.

In Mark's Gospel, at his baptism, Jesus sees the heavens burst open and the Holy Spirit descend on him; he is filled with the Holy Spirit; a voice from heaven clarifies what has happened: "You are my son, the beloved one, in you I am pleased" (v. 11). At that moment, through the descent of the Spirit on Jesus and the voice from heaven, Jesus becomes the Son of God, and from that moment on in the Gospel of Mark, there is no question about his mission to overcome the evil forces that oppress humanity. The evil spirit whom he drives out in the synagogue in Capernaum immediately recognizes this: "What is there between you and us, Jesus of Nazareth? You came to destroy us. I know who you are, the holy one of God" (1:23).

The words spoken by the voice are quoted from Psalm 2:7, "You are my son," followed by a quotation from Isaiah 42:1, "The beloved one, in you I am pleased." The latter appears in a version that we know only in a Greek translation, quoted more fully by Matthew in 12:18–21.

Because Mark's story of Jesus' baptism fits his Gospel so well, it is not possible to distinguish between what Mark quoted and the emphases he himself may have brought to the story. It is also difficult to determine exactly where Matthew and Luke depended on Mark or what interdependence there may have been between the two of them. At a number of points either Matthew or Luke, or both of them, agrees with Mark, and in two cases Matthew and Luke agree with each other against Mark; the heavens "split open" in Mark, but they "open up" in Matthew and Luke (cf. Mark 1:10, //s), and the Greek word for "on" at the end of that verse reads *eis* in Mark, but *ep'* in Matthew and Luke. Each evangelist has his own introduction.

Luke agrees literally with Mark in the words spoken by the voice from heaven, "You are my son, the beloved one, with you I am pleased" (Mark 1:11, //), which suggests that he depended on Mark for the formulation. The formulation of an installation as Son of God does not fit well with his story of the divine generation. It is possible to argue that Matthew changed the words from the *pronouncement* of Jesus as God's son—"You are my son," as we have it in Mark and Luke—to an *announcement* that he was God's son, "This is my son, the beloved one, with whom I am pleased" (v. 17), because the Markan pronouncement conflicted with his understanding that Jesus had already been born the son of God (cf. 1:18–25). However, the heavy dependence on Isaiah 42:1 for the words spoken by the voice from heaven makes it also possible that Matthew's version may have been more original and that Mark made the changes to suit his version of the story as an illumination of Jesus.

Matthew and Luke agree in presenting what happened as an event that concerned all who were present and not, as in Mark, an almost private experience of Jesus. In Matthew especially, the incident is presented as having been intended specifically for the benefit of those present; it is they who are addressed by the voice. Luke's version is less explicit. He does focus on Jesus with the statement that Jesus prayed before the heavens opened (v. 21), but the voice from heaven, even though addressed to Jesus, could equally well have been for the benefit of the others present. That Jesus prays is a typical feature in Luke, encountered repeatedly in his Gospel. Matthew has an additional scene, the argument between Jesus and John on the necessity of John baptizing Jesus (vv. 14–15).

It is impossible to determine whether the three synoptic evangelists depended on a single tradition of the story or on more than one. The parallel story in John 1:19–24, however, shows that the revelation of Jesus as the Son of God at his baptism did exist in more than one tradition. The Johannine version agrees with Matthew in presenting the tradition, not as a story of the illumination of Jesus, but as a revelation to those present that he was the Son of God. In the Fourth Gospel, however, the incident was for the specific benefit of John the Baptist and not really anyone else. The Fourth Gospel presents, in John the Baptist's own words, his ignorance about Jesus' identity until the incident occurred: "He who sent me to baptize with water, it was he who said to me, 'On whom you see the spirit descend, and remain on him, he is the one who baptizes with the Holy Spirit.' And I saw, and witness, that he is the Son of God" (John 1:33–34).

It should be noted that at the time of his baptism Jesus did not yet have disciples; the first disciples were called afterward (cf. Mark 1:16–20, //; #34, and Luke 5:1–11; #41). This is important to remember in view of the disciples' ignorance about Jesus in the Gospels and especially at the transfiguration on the mountain, which was for them not the repetition of an event in which they had been involved earlier. What Jesus alone experienced at his baptism was revealed only then to the three disciples who were present at the transfiguration on the mountain. This makes understandable the distinction in that story between, on the one hand, Jesus, Moses, and Elijah who conversed together, already initiated into the mystery of Jesus' identity, and, on the other, the disciples who experienced it for the first time with fear and incomprehension.

All we can infer historically from the different versions of this story is that Jesus was baptized by John. The implication of this is that at some stage Jesus had probably participated in the **apocalyptically** oriented movement of John. The relationship between John and Jesus is of central importance for an understanding of Jesus and will be discussed extensively below. The temptation of Jesus follows immediately on his baptism in all three synoptic accounts, even though Luke inserted his genealogy between the two events.

2. THE TEMPTATION (MARK 1:12–13, //s; #20)

According to the tradition, subsequent to his baptism Jesus was forced out into the desert to be tested with temptations. Such a testing is not specifically messianic. Similar legends are told about other great religious figures as well, such as Buddha, Zarathustra, and also many lesser persons, such as Christian saints. The Markan account is brief, stating only that Jesus was tempted for forty days, ending with the angels serving him. Note, however, that Mark continues the powerful expression of the event. In Matthew "Jesus was *led* into the desert by the Spirit to be tempted by the devil" (Matt. 4:1), and in Luke, "Filled with the Holy Spirit Jesus *turned* from the Jordan, and was *led* by the Spirit in the desert" (Luke 4:1). Mark, however, reads, "And immediately the Spirit *cast* [*ekballei*, literally "threw out," in the Greek] him into the desert" (Mark 1:12). The violence of Mark's account conforms with the power of the event that had just preceded at Jesus' baptism; it contrasts strongly with the mild description of Matthew and Luke.

The Matthean and Lukan accounts agree with Mark in a number of formulations, but those agreements concern features that are so general that it is not possible to conclude whether Matthew and Luke depended on Mark or found the same information in the sources from which they quoted their longer stories. Matthew and Luke narrate three temptations to which Satan subjected Jesus. There is a large degree of verbal agreement between their accounts, but this could be attributed to the quotations from Scripture, which constitute the largest parts of the stories. A major difference between them is the order of the second and third temptations, but either evangelist could have been responsible for changing the order, Matthew in order to climax the series with the temptation to worship Satan, or, more probably, Luke in order to conclude the temptation in Jerusalem.

There is nothing specifically Christian about the temptations. Their Jewish (or Jewish Christian) origin is clearly manifest in the fencing with quotations from Scripture, a typically rabbinic technique.

In Jesus' baptism by John, and in his relationship to that ascetic preacher, we encounter events in the life of Jesus that may be of the greatest importance for an understanding of him. Before turning to the crucial relationship between Jesus and John the Baptist we should focus briefly on the Gospel headings as the final form in which the traditions about Jesus came down to us.

F. THE GOSPEL HEADINGS (MARK 1:1; LUKE 1:1–4; CF. MATT. 1:1; #1)

The Gospel of Matthew has no heading. It begins with a heading for his genealogy, "The book of the genealogy of Jesus Christ, the son of David, the son of Abraham" (1:1), which extends to 1:17. As we have seen, Matthew links the genealogy with the divine generation story (1:18–25) and the other infancy narratives (2:1–23) by means of the Greek catchword *genesis*, which means "descent" or "genealogy" in 1:1, but "birth" in 1:18. The first part of his Gospel extends to 4:17, with which the transition is made to the actual ministry of Jesus: "From then Jesus started to proclaim, and he said, 'Repent, for the kingdom of God is at hand,'" the exact words pronounced by John in his proclamation (cf. 3:1). The first part of Matthew's Gospel can thus be divided into two main sections: the genealogy and birth and infancy narratives (1:1–2:23), and the activity of Jesus in the context of the proclamation of John the Baptist (3:1–4:16). The first section culminates with the move to Nazareth (2:22–23), the second with the move from Nazareth to Capernaum (4:12–16). We have noted above the structural similarity between these two sections. This first part of the Gospel represents the period of preparation. John's importance in this preparation is indicated by the fact that it is his arrest that prompts Jesus' move from Nazareth to Capernaum (cf. 4:12–14). That move then marks the beginning of Jesus' own proclamation (4:17).

Luke begins his Gospel with a typical Greek prologue, for which there are parallels in the literature of that time, as there are for its repetition at the beginning of his second writing (Acts 1:1, cf., for example, Josephus, *Against Apion* 1.1.1 and 2.1.1). That the dedication to a single person, Theophilus in the case of Luke, does not indicate that it is a private communication is indicated by what Josephus writes in *Against Apion* 2.41.296: "For you then, Epaphroditus, and through you for those who are similarly desirous to know about our nation, I wrote this book and the one before it." Josephus's intention is very similar to that expressed by Luke in the prologue to the Gospel, that is, to give a historically reliable account. It is not known whether Theophilus was a real or a fictitious person.

Only Mark's Gospel has something that could be called a heading: "The *arche* of the gospel of Jesus Christ" (Mark 1:1). *Arche* is usually translated "beginning," which then raises the question how far into the Gospel this beginning extends. However, Mark almost certainly does not use the term *gospel* as a reference to his own writing. The designation *gospel* for these writings is relatively late. Matthew uses the term for (the proclamation of) "the good tidings" of the kingdom of God (4:23; 24:14; 26:13), and Paul uses it for the proclamation of salvation through Christ Jesus, for example, in Galatians 1:6–12, and Romans 1:16–17. The Greek term *arche* does not mean beginning in the sense of what comes first, but more fundamentally that out of which everything else emerges. The *arche* of the gospel of Jesus Christ should probably be understood as the "source" of the gospel of Jesus Christ. Mark's writing itself is the *arche*, the source out of which the gospel, the proclamation of salvation in Christ Jesus, emerged. In it he wants to clarify the basis on which salvation in Christ was proclaimed, namely, that Jesus was the messiah, the Son of God, the meaning of which came to its fullest expression in his passion and resurrection.

Conclusion. The stories of the divine generation of Jesus; the legends of his birth in Bethlehem as a descendant of David, reinforced by the Matthean and Lukan genealogies, which trace his descent back to David and beyond; the story of his rejection in Nazareth; and the controversies about his messiahship in the question concerning the messiah's sonship of David express the impression that Jesus made on his followers. We are left only with an impression of his significance, which is important in itself. The question that arises, however, is how it happened that he made such an impression on those who became his followers. He himself had evidently been similarly impressed by John the Baptist, whose disciple he must have been at some stage, as signified by his baptism. His complex relationship to the ascetic desert preacher may provide an important clue to who he was and why his significance was not shattered by his execution as a messianic pretender but grew, as the motivating power from which emerged a religion that spread beyond the boundaries of Palestine to the limits of the Roman empire and in due course to the entire world. Central to the way he was remembered was his association with the social and religious outcasts, an attitude that he shared with the Galilean holy men Hanina and Honi. But through his death and what followed from it, he became more than an example for such behavior; he became the symbol for it. Through his death Jesus became the symbol for what he represented in word and deed during his lifetime.

Jesus' relationship with John appears to have been decisive. It is a relationship that may help us understand what made him, through his death, become the symbol for what he represented before his death. Who Jesus was was not determined by his relationship to John, but that relationship demanded that he make a choice in lifestyle that sheds important light on the kind of person he was. At the same time, even after he had broken with John's way of life, the closeness of his relationship with this remarkable figure appears not to have lost its significance.

CHAPTER 2

John the Baptist and Jesus

Of the few facts concerning Jesus about which we can be relatively certain, his relationship to John the Baptist, may promise the fullest answer the question of who he was. Up to this point we have established that Jesus grew up in Nazareth and was baptized by John. In order to learn as much as possible from the relationship between Jesus and John, it is first necessary to establish what we can know about John. Our information contains legends about his birth and traditions about his ministry.

A. THE BIRTH OF JOHN, HIS MINISTRY AND DEATH (LUKE 1:5–25, 39–80; MARK 1:2–8, //s; LUKE 3:7–9, //; 3:10–14; MARK 6:17–29, //; LUKE 3:19–20)

The present form of the traditions about the birth and ministry of John are heavily influenced by the Christian understanding of him as the forerunner of Jesus. Nevertheless, it is still possible to recognize behind these traditions a conception of him that is quite contrary to that provided by New Testament Christianity.

1. THE BIRTH STORIES (LUKE 1:5–25, 39–80; #2 and 4–5)

The first chapter of Luke consists of four stories: the announcement of the birth of John (vv. 5–25), the announcement of the birth of Jesus (vv. 26–38), Mary's visit to Elizabeth (vv. 39–56), and the birth of John (vv. 57–80). These stories relate the births of John and Jesus to each other in a way that clearly makes Jesus the more important of the two. The series of stories continues into the second chapter of the Gospel, which we already discussed above. We also discussed the story of the announcement of the birth of Jesus (Luke 1:26–38). What remains to be discussed, thus, are the stories of the announcement of John's birth, Mary's visit to Elizabeth, and

31

the birth of John. Of these, the story of Mary's visit to Elizabeth is clearly of Christian origin, establishing Jesus as the greater of the two figures. As we will see, however, the Magnificat may originally have been a psalm from the circle of John's disciples.

The Magnificat (vv. 46–55) and the Benedictus of Zechariah (vv. 68–79) are independent psalms that fit rather loosely in their present settings. It is easy to see that the Magnificat has been fitted secondarily into the story of Mary's visit to Elizabeth. The introduction of Mary as subject in verse 56, "And Mary stayed with her," presupposes that not she, but Elizabeth is the subject of the previous sentence. Verse 46, however, already introduced Mary as the subject who pronounced the Magnificat. In verse 56 one would thus expect, "And she stayed with Elizabeth." In its present form we have to reach further back to find Elizabeth as the subject, that is, to verses 42–45. All this leads to the conclusion that verses 46–55 were evidently added later. The Magnificat is, in any case, more applicable to Elizabeth than to Mary. It is Elizabeth's situation that recalls that of Hannah, the mother of Samuel, who is quoted in verse 48, "He looked upon the lowness of his maid" (1 Sam. 1:11). Hannah's psalm after the birth of Samuel (cf. 1 Sam. 2:1–10) is also recalled by the Magnificat.

Turning now to the stories of the announcement (vv. 5–25) and the birth of John (vv. 57–66) we can note a very close connection between them. Everything predicted in the story of the announcement comes to pass in that of the birth. They appear to have been an original unity separated now by the stories of the announcement of the birth of Jesus and of Mary's visit to Elizabeth. The story of John is typical of stories in the Hebrew Scriptures of the birth of a child through God's intervention to a woman who was barren and already beyond the age of childbearing, for example the births of Samson (Judg. 13:2–14), Samuel (1 Sam. 1 and 2), and Isaac (Gen. 18:1–15; 21:1–7).

According to the announcement of John's birth, John was to receive the Spirit while he was still in his mother's womb (v. 15). He was also to be an ascetic, a feature that was taken from the prescriptions for a Nazirite in Numbers 6:3 (cf. Judg. 13:4–5, 1 Sam. 1:11). However, nothing appears in any of the traditions to suggest that his head was not shaved, another requirement for a Nazirite, so we cannot assume that John was a Nazirite. The tradition also states that John was to proceed before God in the spirit and power of Elijah to bring about a reconciliation within Israel and so prepare the people for God's own coming. Note that "go before him" in verse 17 refers back to "the Lord, their God" in verse 16. According to this tradition, therefore, John was the forerunner of God himself, not of Jesus. In the expectations expressed in these verses there is no place for another eschatological figure between John and God's own coming. John was the final eschatological figure. We may conclude from this that the tradition of John's birth did not originate in Christian circles, but in the circles of John's followers. (These circles were making claims for him similar to those made for Jesus by Christians.) This is confirmed by certain features of the Benedictus of Zechariah.

As indicated above, the Benedictus of Zechariah has two parts, a more general one, which could have applied to any political messianic figure (vv. 68–75), and a more specific one, which applies specifically to John (vv. 76–79). The first part is characterized by a heavy political tone, the deliverance of Israel from its enemies. There are no other indications anywhere else in the Gospel traditions that John was a political messianic pretender. However, according to the **Pseudo-Clementine** *Recognitions* 1. 60, "One of the disciples of John claimed John to have been the messiah, and not Jesus, 'in so far as,' he said, 'Jesus himself pronounced John greater than all men and prophets.' " It is not absolutely necessary to understand *messiah* in a political sense in this saying. However, according to Josephus, Herod did indeed have John executed because he was afraid that John's great influence could lead to "some kind of a revolt" (*Antiquities of the Jews* 18. 116–119). It was a fear similar to what the Jewish authorities in Jerusalem harbored about Jesus, as we will see below. We will return to the Josephus account below in connection with the death of John.

It is the second part of the Benedictus, however, that places John fully in competition with Jesus. Verses 78–79 refer to John as "the rising from above which will shine on those who dwell in darkness and in the shadow of death." This is a quotation from Isaiah 9:1, which is also quoted in connection with Jesus in Matthew 4:16, "The people dwelling in darkness saw a great light, and to those who dwell in the land and the shadow of death a light went up." John's followers were obviously claiming the same things for him as the Christians were claiming for Jesus. The polemic between them also comes to expression in the statement of the fourth evangelist that John "was not the light, but he came in order to witness concerning the light" (John 1:8).

In the Benedictus John is presented, not as the figure of judgment he is usually thought to have been, but as someone who brought forgiveness and reconciliation with God. In verse 76 allusions to Malachi 3:1 and Isaiah 40:3 are combined to present him as the expected prophet who was to prepare the way for God's coming. We will encounter these allusions again in the Christian tradition, but there they are reinterpreted as references to the coming of Jesus, not God (cf. esp. Mark 1:2–3, //s).

The Magnificat, as we indicated above, is a psalm that originally expressed joy about Elizabeth's situation. It does not contribute anything to our understanding of either John or Jesus except that, as a psalm concerning the circumstances of Elizabeth, it presents John's mother as one who had been barren and beyond the normal age of childbearing when she gave birth.

Luke made these traditions about John subservient to the Christian perspective by placing them in the context of the story of Mary's visit to Elizabeth (vv. 39–56). In that way he was able to use them as arguments in favor of the Christian viewpoint against that of John's disciples from whom they originated. By leaving these traditions and psalms unchanged Luke ensured their maximum effect as Christian propaganda, especially among John's followers. By having the unborn John recognize the superiority of the unborn Jesus (v. 41), John's secondary status in relation to Jesus is already established. John expresses the same relationship when he says, "He must become greater and I should diminish in importance" (John 3:30). Matthias Grünewald's painting accurately represents this Christian understanding of the Gospels: John points with his elongated forefinger in a gesture that says, "There is the lamb of God who takes away the sins of the world" (John 1:29). As we will see, this probably does not represent Jesus' own understanding of the relationship between himself and John. What is more important, it is doubtful that we would be able to understand who Jesus really was as long as his predecessor is relegated to this position of a mere forerunner.

The picture we get of John in the traditions of his followers (as preserved in Luke) is not of a forerunner of Jesus, but of the final eschatological figure who prepared the way for God's own coming. He acted in the spirit and power of Elijah (v. 17, cf. 76), representing not judgment but forgiveness and reconciliation of the people with each other and with God (vv. 14–17, 76–79). According to these traditions John's ministry truly represented the good tidings of God's coming to the people. But what then did Jesus represent? We will find an answer to that question only when we have investigated further who John was.

2. JOHN'S MINISTRY (MARK 1:2–8, //S; LUKE 3:7–9, 3:10–14, //)

We may discard from the outset the general, practical directives quoted in Luke 3:10–14 (#15) as historically not very informative about John. They may not even have come from John. It is highly improbably that John would have been called upon to give the rather mild, commonsense moral directives of verse 14 to soldiers, whom one would also not expect to have sought advice from an ascetic preacher in the desert bordering on the Jordan. The advice in this passage could have come from almost any moral preacher of the time.

Strikingly different is the harsh, general threat of imminent judgment in Luke 3:7–9, // (#14). Matthew qualifies the threat by making it apply specifically to the Pharisees and Sadducees (v. 7). Aside from this difference in Matthew's introductory statement, he and Luke reproduce the tradition with almost complete verbal agreement. It is important to note that the threat of eschatological judgment in this passage is duplicated in the proclamation of Jesus in Luke 11:31–32 (#191) and 13:28–29 (#210), in the woes of the Sermon on the Plain (Luke 6:24–25, #79), and especially in the speech against the scribes and Pharisees in Matthew 23:1–36 (#284). In all of these the judgment is a reversal of what was expected, emphasized in Luke 13:28–29 by the addition of an independent saying, "The last will be first, and the first will be last" (v. 30). Matthew quotes the same saying in a different context in 19:30. The same kind of reversal is expressed in the present passage by the rejection of the claim of being a child of Abraham (Luke 3:8, //).

This passage with its prediction of eschatological doom contrasts sharply with the nationalistic expectations of the first part of the Benedictus (esp. 1:73), and even more so with the promise of reconciliation and forgiveness in the second part (vv. 77–79). It also contrasts with the angel's announcement of John's birth (v. 16), and with what is said in verses 54–55 of the Magnificat. It is, of course, not impossible for a radical preacher to coordinate the threat of imminent wrath with the promise of reconciliation. The coordination of the beatitudes and woes in the Sermon on the Plain (Luke 6:21–26) is an example of such a procedure. Other examples can be found in Luke 10:15; 12:8–9; and Matthew 10:32–33. It is nevertheless remarkable that in connection with John each aspect has been remembered so separately from the other.

That sayings such as Luke 3:7–9, // occur elsewhere in the Gospels in the mouth of Jesus indicates that they did not necessarily originate from John. Note in particular the similarity in tone of John's first saying, "Offspring of vipers, who has shown you to flee from the coming wrath?" (Matt. 3:7b), and the saying of Jesus in Matthew 23:33, "Serpents, offspring of vipers, how will you flee from the judgment of gehenna?" We can neither attribute any of these sayings with certainty to John, nor can we assume that any one in particular did not come from him. Certain answers concerning the origin of these sayings elude historical inquiry.

The juxtaposition of a message of reconciliation and a threat of dire judgment can also be discerned behind the tradition of Matthew 3:11–12, //. Note also a partial parallel in Mark 1:7–8 (#16). The saying makes two distinguishable points: first, that someone greater than John comes after him (Mark 1:7, //s, cf. John 1:27), and then that John's baptism with water will be followed by a contrasting eschatological baptism with the Spirit and with fire (Mark 1:8, //s). The two points are separable. The fourth evangelist includes only the saying concerning the greater one who is to follow and nothing about the contrast between the two forms of baptism (cf. John 1:26–27). This is all the more significant since he also mentions John's baptism with water in the same context. Furthermore, in the present passage the saying concerning the greater one who is to follow is placed differently in Mark (before the two contrasting forms of baptism) than in Matthew and Luke (between the two forms of baptism), another indication of the original independence of the saying.

The saying concerning the greater one who is to follow is clearly of Christian origin and again places John in a position secondary to Jesus. To emphasize the christological point, Luke places it in the context of speculation about John's messiahship. The crowds wonder about John, "Maybe he is the messiah" (3:15). In that way what John says becomes a denial of the claim that he is the messiah, similar to the fourth evangelist's statement in 1:20, "And he [John] affirmed, and he did not deny, but affirmed, 'I am not the Christ.' " Luke's statement confirms that there must have been speculation that he had been the messiah.

Remarkable about the second contrasting form of baptism is the combination of the Holy Spirit, with its salvific meaning, and fire, which is the fire of eschatological judgment, as the exposition in Matthew 3:13, // reveals. The fire consumes everything that is impure, as in 1 Corinthians 3:13, "The works of each will be brought to light; for the day will let it be exposed, because it will be revealed in fire, and the nature of the works of each will be tested by fire." John's baptism is presented here as mild, but that which is to come with Jesus is severe.

That baptism with the Holy Spirit and with fire do not necessarily go together is indicated by the absence of the combination in Mark, who speaks of only the baptism with the Holy Spirit. Did Mark delete the reference to the baptism with fire because it presented Jesus as a figure of judgment, which was contrary to his understanding of him? Note in this regard John 3:17–18, "God did not send his son to judge the world, but to save the world through him. Whoever believes in him is not judged, but whoever does not believe is already condemned because he [she] did not believe in the name of the only begotten Son of God." According to this passage those who did not believe in the Son of God condemned themselves with the very act of rejecting. Did Mark have a similar view and therefore remove the reference to the baptism with the fire of eschatological judgment? As we will see, there is a better explanation for the differences in the synoptic versions of what John said.

Mark's contrast between the baptism of John and Jesus' coming baptism with the Holy Spirit without mention of fire has a parallel in Acts 19:1–8. The disciples encountered by Paul in Ephesus had been baptized only with John's baptism; they had not yet received the Holy Spirit. Paul explained to them: " 'John baptized a baptism of repentance which announced to the people the one coming after him with the purpose that they should believe in him.' And when they heard this they were baptized in the name of the Lord Jesus; and, Paul placing his hands on them, the Holy Spirit came upon them" (vv. 4–6). The reference to the "split tongues as if of fire" that appeared on the heads of the disciples when they received the Holy Spirit (Acts 2:3) is not a baptism with fire in the sense of our passage or of 1 Corinthians 3:13, although the tongues of fire, representing a divine presence (cf. the apocryphal 1 Enoch 14:8–15 and 71:5), may have represented the disciples' security against the coming of such a baptism with the fire of eschatological judgment.

The contrast between John's baptism of repentance and reconciliation and the coming judgment with fire is probably of a pre-Christian origin, originally without reference to baptism with the Holy Spirit. It probably presented John's baptism as the preparation for God's coming judgment,

as in Luke 3:7–9, and its parallel, Matthew 23:33. God also acts as an un-
merciful eschatological judge in Matthew 22:13. As the allegorical king
who encounters the guest without a wedding garment, symbolizing his
lack of preparation, he commands his servants, "Tie his feet and hands
and cast him into the darkest darkness. There will be wailing and a gnashing of teeth."

We may be able to uncover the process by which the salvific baptism
with the Holy Spirit and baptism with the fire of eschatological judgment
became combined if we consider the relationships between the three versions of the present story of what John said. With regard to the Markan
version: The Acts 19 passage reveals that the contrast between John's baptism and baptism with the Holy Spirit did not necessarily involve a baptism
with fire. Thus there is no need to assume that Mark eliminated the reference to baptism with fire; he may have encountered the tradition in the
form in which he reproduced it here without mentioning a baptism with
fire. Indeed, the association of baptism with fire and with the Holy Spirit
may be secondary.

Luke's dependence on Mark in the passage is indicated by his complete
verbal agreement with Mark's "to untie the straps of his sandals" (v. 16, cf.
Mark 1:7), against Matthew's "to carry his sandals" (v. 11). The reference
to baptism with the Holy Spirit in all three versions (Mark 1:8, //s) thus
appears to be due to Matthew's and Luke's dependence on Mark. The Q
tradition quoted by Matthew and Luke probably contrasted John's baptism only with the baptism with fire. It could have originated in the circles
of John as a tradition about his preaching in which his baptism of repentance and reconciliation was contrasted with God's baptism with the fire of
eschatological judgment, including the continuation in Luke 3:17, //.

When New Testament Christianity came to understand Jesus as the one
for whom John prepared the way, Jesus also took the place of God as the
one who would baptize with fire. That prepared the way for Matthew and
Luke to combine the tradition of Mark 1:7–8 with their Q tradition. In
this way Jesus' baptism with the Holy Spirit became incongruously associated with an eschatological baptism with fire. The result was that John
now appeared as the milder, reconciling figure and Jesus as a severe
judge. That image of Jesus is not altogether absent in the Gospel tradition,
for example, in the description of the last judgment (Matt. 25:31–46) he is
presented as follows: "When the Son of Man will come in his glory and all
his angels with him, he will sit on his throne of glory, and all the nations of
the world will be brought before him, and he will separate them from each
other as a shepherd separates the sheep from the goats" (vv. 31–32).

With regard to Mark 1:2–6, //s (#16): It is difficult, if not impossible, to
unravel the history of this passage's tradition. On the one hand, Matthew
and Luke agree with each other against Mark in placing the quotation of
Isaiah 40:3 after the statement that John baptized in the desert, preaching
a baptism of repentance (Matt. 3:1–4, //). In Mark the quotation precedes

the statement about John (Mark 1:3). Matthew and Luke also agree against Mark in not quoting the combination of Exodus 23:20 and Malachi 3:1 at this stage (cf. Mark 3:2) but at the same location later in their Gospels (Matt. 11:10, //). All three Gospels agree verbally in the quotation of Isaiah 40:3, including the change from "make straight the paths of my God" at the end of the verse to "make straight his paths," by means of which the quotation was made applicable to Jesus.

On the other hand, in rendering the actual tradition, that is, apart from the quotations, Matthew and Luke never agree with each other against Mark. Luke agrees substantially with Mark against Matthew in the parallel to Mark 1:4 (cf. Luke 3:2–3), but he has nothing that parallels Mark 1:5–6. In the case of the latter verses, however, Matthew agrees substantially with Mark, except that he includes some of the material in an inverted order. (Compare Matt. 3:5–6 and 4, respectively, with Mark 1:5 and 6.) Luke introduces the passage with historical information that places the beginning of the activity of John within the framework of world history. He gives a longer quotation from Isaiah 40, which includes verses 4–5. Although some dependence on Mark seems indicated, it remains unclear why both Matthew and Luke changed the placement of the Isaiah quotation and why neither has the Exodus/Malachi quotation at this point. One can speculate about this, but conclusive results remain unobtainable.

The only evidence of a Christian point of view in the present form of this tradition is the change of the end of the quotation of Isaiah 40:3 from "make straight the paths of my God" to "make straight his paths" in all three versions (Mark 1:3, //s), the implied reference to Jesus in the second person singular pronoun *your* in the Exodus quotation, and the change of the first person singular pronoun "my" of Malachi 3:1 to the second person "your," by means of which the quotation is made applicable to Jesus (Mark 1:2). Except for these changes or additions the tradition could just as easily have originated in the circles of John's followers. In its original form it presented John as the final eschatological figure preparing the way for God's own coming. Even the quotation of Isaiah 40:3 could have been part of this original tradition, that is, before a Christian hand changed "make straight the paths of my God" of the Isaiah text to "make straight his paths."

The clothing John wore and the food he ate (Mark 1:6) were characteristic of the poor in the desert. His presence in the desert, however, was significant in Jewish thought, because the desert symbolized the place where one expected to meet God. That John baptized in the Jordan but lived and preached in the desert does not have to be contradictory, if he operated in the lower part of the Jordan valley, the borders of which were considered desert in the biblical world.

3. JOHN'S DEATH (MARK 6:17–29, //; #144; CF. LUKE 3:19–20; #17)

Two distinctly different versions record the death of John, the Gospel tradition and Josephus's account to which we referred above (*Antiquities*

18.116–19). According to Josephus, Herod had John executed because
he feared that John's great influence would lead to an uprising. Josephus
also reports a connection between John and Herodias, but an entirely different one from that in the Gospels. Herod had previously been married
to the daughter of Aretas, the Nabataean king, whom he abandoned
when he married Herodias. In revenge Aretas attacked and destroyed
Herod's army, an act that the Jews interpreted as God's punishment of
Herod for the execution of John. According to Josephus, Herodias was
the wife of Herod's stepbrother (also named Herod) and not the wife of
his brother Philip, as Mark states (6:17). Philip's involvement is through
his marriage to Salome, Herodias's daughter by her previous marriage.
These incidents and relations appear to have supplied abundant material
for the type of colorful novelette contained in the Markan tradition. The
only thing that appears certain from all the accounts is that John was imprisoned and executed on the orders of Herod.

The Markan version is a colorful story containing human interest details. Matthew apparently quoted from Mark but with considerable abbre-
viation. Luke left out the story of John's death, although he followed
Mark both before and after the story. Luke may have left out the story, at
least in part, because he had already mentioned John's imprisonment—
but not his death—in a brief statement earlier in his Gospel (3:19–20). He
may also have considered the story improbable. He does agree with Mark,
however, that John was imprisoned because he had criticized Herod's
marriage to his brother's wife, Herodias. Note, however, that Luke does
not identify the brother as Philip, a detail that is contradicted by Josephus.

Conclusion. Notwithstanding the strong tendency of the Gospel traditions to present John as a figure whose significance was limited to being a
forerunner of Jesus, we can recognize behind these traditions another image of John as the final eschatological figure who was preparing the way
for God's own coming to the people. John appears to have been an ascetic
who withdrew into the desert from the sinful world, preaching forgiveness and reconciliation in the face of the imminent judgment on those
who were unprepared for God's coming. The impression we get, especially from the story of his birth and the psalms associated with it, is that
his preaching was characterized by the message of forgiveness and reconciliation even though its backdrop was the threat of imminent doom. He
baptized those who were persuaded by his preaching as a rite of purification from sin.

The tendency of Christians to place John in a subservient position
reached its culmination in the Fourth Gospel in which John's baptism was
reduced to a screening process by means of which he was able to recognize
Jesus. When John was asked, "Why do you baptize if you are neither the
messiah nor Elijah nor the prophet?" (1:25), he replied, "I baptize with
water, but among you there is someone whom you do not know who
comes after me, of whom I am not worthy to untie the strap of his sandal"

(vv. 26–27). The reply is concluded only later in the chapter when he says, "I also did not know him, but in order that he should be revealed to Israel, for that reason did I come baptizing with water. . . . He who sent me to baptize with water said to me, 'He on whom you see the Spirit descend and remain, is the one who baptizes with the Holy Spirit' " (vv. 31, 33).

This relatively low estimation of John in the Gospel traditions was not shared by Jesus, whose regard for him was similar to that of John's own disciples. Jesus' high regard for John probably prevented New Testament Christianity from showing real hostility toward him, notwithstanding the controversies that existed between themselves and John's followers. To Jesus' own understanding of John we now turn our attention.

B. JOHN AND JESUS (MARK 9:1, 11–13; 11:27–33, //s; MATT. 11:2–19, //)

In the Gospel traditions the image of John the Baptist fell prey to the christological self-interest of the primitive church, aggravated by the polemics with John's followers. We have seen that behind some of the traditions quoted by the evangelists the views of John's own followers are still recognizable. They represent an understanding of John quite contrary to that of the Gospels themselves. This is particularly true of the traditions that we are about to discuss.

1. JOHN, THE RETURNING ELIJAH (MARK 9:1, 11–13, //s; #160, 162)

Mark 9:1, 11–13 probably formed an original unity into which Mark wove the story of the transfiguration (Mark 9:2–10). The disciples' question in verse 11 presupposes a statement concerning the coming of the kingdom of God such as the one found in 9:1. The formulation in verse 1, "There are some of those present here who will not taste death before they see the kingdom of God coming in power," affirms the conviction that (at least) some of those present will still be alive at the coming of the kingdom of God. It presupposes the experience of a delay in Christ's **parousia** and so also in the coming of the kingdom of God, here projected back into the life of Jesus and connected to speculation concerning the return of Elijah.

Jesus affirms the expectation that Elijah had to come first but insists that he had already come and that "they did to him whatever they wanted, as was written about him," an evident reference to the death of John. Yet, nothing in Scripture suggests that the returning Elijah was to suffer. The question about the Son of Man has been inserted into Jesus' reply quite crudely, "And how was it written about the Son of Man that he must suffer much and be rejected?" There is also no reference in Scripture for the suffering of the Son of Man. However, *Son of Man* here probably simply means Jesus, and since the New Testament Christians understood that everything about Jesus had been predicted in Scripture, *Son of Man* could be used even if no scriptural reference could be located.

Mark 9:1, 11–13 concerns the delay in the parousia of Jesus. Verse 1 holds on to the expectation that the coming of the kingdom of God is still at hand; it expresses the conviction that at least some of those present would still see the coming of the kingdom of God. Verses 11–13 answer the objection, quoted here as coming from the scribes, that Elijah must return before the kingdom of God could come. The answer to the objection is that Elijah had already returned in the person of John. It should be noted that even in the present form the saying presents John as the one who prepared the way for the coming of the kingdom of God, not for Jesus. Jesus is involved only by implication, and then not in terms of his earthly activity—as in the traditions discussed in the previous section (especially Mark 1:2–8, //s)—but of his return as the Son of Man ushering in the kingdom of God.

Matthew and Luke apparently depended on Mark for their versions of 9:1. Except for individual changes, both follow Mark quite closely, never agreeing with each other against him. Matthew turned the saying about the coming of the kingdom of God into an explicit reference to the parousia of Jesus. Luke, however, probably aware that the parousia did not occur in the lifetime of any of Jesus' followers, changed the reference to a more general way of experiencing the kingdom, with no specific connection to the parousia of Jesus as Son of Man.

Matthew also followed Mark quite closely in his version of Mark 9:11–13. The main difference is that he moved the crude placement of the statement concerning the suffering of the Son of Man farther down, placing it after Jesus' assertion that Elijah had already come and that they did to him whatever they wanted. He also added the explicit identification of John with Elijah, as he did previously in 11:14. Luke left out the entire passage and nowhere explicitly identified John with Elijah. In 1:17 he only quoted the angel as saying that John would come "in the spirit and power of Elijah." Was this because he knew that if John had been the returning Elijah, the final eschatological figure before the coming of the kingdom of God, there would have been no place for Jesus? As we have seen, the fourth evangelist has John explicitly deny that he is the returning Elijah (1:21, cf. 25).

Even though Mark may have encountered the sayings in 9:1 and 11–13 as a single tradition, they do not necessarily belong together. Mark 9:1 could originally have stood on its own; it requires nothing after it, as in Luke. And if one then takes 9:11–13 independently of 9:1, it would appear that the question concerning Elijah's return was posed against the assertion that the kingdom of God was at hand, without regard to the return of Jesus. Indeed, the question is formulated as a response to the assertion that the kingdom had already come: how can one claim that the kingdom of God has already arrived when the scribes say that Elijah has to come first? That assertion may have been replaced by the present statement in verse 1, reformulating it in the context of the delay in the parousia. Jesus' reply affirms the reasoning of the scribes. He claims, however, that Elijah had already come and that the preparation for the coming of the kingdom of God was already complete.

2. THE AUTHORITY OF JOHN AND OF JESUS (MARK 11:27–33, //s; #276)

Mark 11:28–30 is a rabbinic dispute in which a question is answered with a counterquestion. To this has been added a second part in which the deliberations of Jesus' questioners lead them to refuse to answer his counterquestion (vv. 31–33b), which in turn causes Jesus to refuse to answer their original question (v. 33c–d). In the present version of the story, Jesus tricks his questioners into providing him with the excuse for not answering their question because he obviously knew that they would refuse to answer him. His counterquestion, thus, is a way of avoiding an answer to their question. It is not surprising that Luke leaves out the part of Jesus' statement in which he said that he would tell them on what authority he did "these things" if they answered his question, since in the present version of the story he obviously never intends to do so (cf. Luke 20:3).

Taken by itself, however, the first part of the story, verses 28–30, does provide an answer to the questioners. In this form of rabbinic dispute, Jesus' counterquestion informs the questioners that they will find the answer to their question by answering the counterquestion: the source of authority for the activity of Jesus and for John's baptism is the same.

The early church did not understand this type of rabbinic exchange, so those who handed down the tradition provided the addition, which was intended to complete the exchange between Jesus and his questioners without changing the intent of the story. In the new version Jesus did not add anything to his original counterquestion, but it became clear that this counterquestion was a way of refusing to answer his questioners.

Except for the introductions, the renditions of this story in all three Gospels are very similar. In a few points Matthew and Luke agree against Mark, but in a number of cases one of them agrees with Mark against the other. They even agree on the location of the story in the Gospels, which probably indicates dependence on Mark. However, Matthew and Luke may also have known the story in other similar versions, which would explain their deviations from Mark, especially those in which they agree against him. The most significant change mentioned above is Luke's omission of Jesus' statement that he would tell his questioners on what authority he did "these things" if they answered his question (cf. Mark 11:29, //s). The context of the story—whether the original or the present version—is unclear. There is no indication to what "these things" refer.

In the original story of the dispute (vv. 28–30) Jesus appeals to the authority of John's baptism to answer the question concerning his own authority. In so doing he allows his own activity to be interpreted within the framework of John's. This is all the more significant since at this stage he evidently was no longer a member of the circle of John's followers. If he had still been, the question concerning his authority would have been unnecessary. According to the story, thus, even when Jesus acted on his own he still understood his activity within the framework of John's. This remarkable state of affairs may have contributed to the misunderstanding of his reply in the Christian tradition according to which Jesus did not act in dependence on John; to the contrary, it was John's activity that derived its meaning from that of Jesus, even though Jesus came after him. The fact that the view presented in the original, first part of this story is so contrary to the Christian understanding suggests that it is very old, and one could at least wonder if it does not go back to Jesus himself. As we are about to see, the understanding of the relationship between John and Jesus in these verses is confirmed by the traditions in Matthew 11:2–19, //.

3. JOHN'S QUESTION AND THE REPLY OF JESUS (MATT. 11:2–19, //; #106–7)

According to Matthew 11:2–6, John the Baptist sent messengers to Jesus to ask if he was the one who was to come or whether they should expect another (vv. 2–3). Jesus gave an indirect answer, referring to the miracles that were being performed in fulfillment of Scripture and pronouncing those blessed who were not scandalized by him. His reply does not really answer whether or not he was the one who was to come (vv. 4–6). Nevertheless, the assumption in the present form of the story is that both John and Jesus knew exactly what John was asking, and that the reply of Jesus, indirect as it was, did answer the question. Such an understanding is unimaginable in an actual historical situation in which the imprisoned John began wondering whether Jesus was indeed "the one who is coming." Also, as we have seen, John probably expected, not another eschatological figure, but the coming of God's kingdom itself. A situation in which Jesus' reply would have been understandable is that of the primitive church, in which it was taken for granted that Jesus was precisely the one whom John expected. Whatever Jesus replied would have been understood as an affirmative answer. We may ask, however, whether an earlier layer is still discernible behind the present form of the tradition. Before answering that question, it would be useful to clarify the history of the tradition of the rest of the passage, according to which, after the departure of John's disciples, Jesus made a short speech with the following parts: (1) An affirmation of John's desert existence against contrary expectations, culminating in the combination of the quotations from Exodus 23:20 and Malachi 3:1 (vv. 7–10); (2) Sayings expressing the great worth of John (vv. 11–15); (3) A parable about children in the market place, which is interpreted as an expression of the contrast between John and Jesus (vv. 16–19).

1. We are already familiar with John's humble mode of existence from Mark 1:6, //, and with the understanding of him as the forerunner of Jesus based on the Christian interpretation of Malachi 3:1, combined with Exodus 23:20 (Mark 1:2, //s). The significance of the present passage is that Jesus defends John's humble existence after he himself had given up that

way of living. His statements challenge anyone who questions John's appearance or mode of existence, culminating in the statement that John was not to be counted among the other prophets because he was more than just another prophet. In its original sense, the quotation of Malachi 3:1 would have identified him as the returning Elijah who had been preparing the way for god's own coming. Only the Christian reformulation, combined with Exodus 23:20, makes him the forerunner of Jesus. Without this Christian reformulation Jesus' reply would have placed John second to no other human being. As we will see, the rest of the passage confirms this understanding.

2. Jesus' statement that "no one born on earth [literally, "of women"] is greater than John the Baptist" (v. 11) puts John second only to heavenly beings. According to the Pseudo-Clementine *Recognitions* (1.60) mentioned earlier, the disciples of John used this saying to argue that John, not Jesus, was the messiah. In the present saying Jesus does indeed affirm that John is the greatest of all persons on earth; by implication, that would include Jesus as well, since he too was born of a woman.

The meaning of the second part of the saying, "But the least in the kingdom of the heavens is greater than he," is ambiguous. It could be a Christian addition, intended to qualify the greatness attributed to John; it asserts that the statement according to which John was greater than all who were born "of women" did not apply to those who belonged to Jesus. Another possible meaning of the second part of the saying is that John's appearance as the returning Elijah brought about a new situation in which the kingdom of God was no longer expected as a future event but seen as inaugurated by John's activity. In this latter sense, the second part of the saying, rather than looking backward as a qualification of the acknowledgment of John's greatness, points forward to participation in the benefits of the kingdom whose coming John as the returning Elijah had ushered in. Great as John was, he still represented the time of expectation, or at the most, of transition. As we shall see below, according to this earlier tradition, Jesus distinguished himself from John because he believed that the kingdom had already become a present reality, whereas John lived in anticipation of its imminence. The second part of the saying, thus, does not detract form the greatness of John expressed in the first but adds to it by pointing to the benefits that had become available as a result of his presence. It suggests that John can be superseded, but only in terms of the time of the kingdom, whether close at hand or already present.

That the kingdom had already arrived is also presupposed by Matthew 11:12–15, for which there is a parallel later in Luke's Gospel (16:16). It is not altogether clear in these verses what is meant by "violating" the kingdom of heaven and "taking possession of it with violence" (v. 12). (The RSV has "the kingdom of heaven has suffered violence, and men of violence take it by force." The Lukan parallel reads "and everyone violates it" [16:16], for which the RSV has "everyone enters it violently.") Whatever is meant by the violence with which the kingdom is attacked, the saying presupposes the presence of the kingdom in such a way that persons could act with violence in relation to it. Verse 13 then states explicitly that the time of the prophets and the Law was concluded with John. Luke adds, "From then on the kingdom of God is proclaimed" (16:16). According to this saying Jesus understood that not he himself but John was the decisive figure ushering in the kingdom of God. It was John who marked the transition between the ages, placing Jesus in the time of the kingdom, which had already arrived. The previous period moved forward toward John, in whose activity it culminated; the period of the kingdom moved forward from John, leaving the time of transition behind. Matthew once more explicitly identifies John with the returning Elijah, an understanding with which we are now quite familiar.

The traditions about Jesus in the synoptic Gospels do not provide a concrete picture of his understanding of the kingdom of God. He would have conceived of it within the framework of the apocalyptic thinking of his time: God's intervention in history for the sake of justice, an intervention surrounded by violent events, such as described in Mark 13, the so-called Little Apocalypse. However, what is decisive for an understanding of Jesus is not *how* he conceived of the kingdom of God, but *that* he understood the activity of John the Baptist as having inaugurated the time of the kingdom, that he lived in a time in which the days of the reign of evil in the world were numbered, and that one should not live with a sense of doom but with the assurance that God's liberation of a suffering humanity had arrived.

After his death, Jesus' followers, unlike Jesus himself understood Jesus rather than John as the eschatological figure whose activity signaled the coming of the kingdom of God. Even more important was that they did not understand the kingdom to have been inaugurated by Jesus' past activity; they expected it to arrive when Jesus returned as the Son of Man, which they referred to as his parousia, not in the sense of the original meaning of "presence," but of his "return." The result is that sayings about the kingdom already present appear in the synoptic tradition along with others that refer to its future coming, giving the impression that the kingdom of God was in some way both present and future in the preaching of Jesus. This is a problem that has plagued some of the best New Testament scholars for a long time. The answer to the problem is that two sets of unrelated sayings concerning the coming of the kingdom of God appear together in the synoptic Gospels: Jesus understood the kingdom of God to have been inaugurated by John the Baptist, which meant that it had already arrived, whereas his followers expected its coming with the return of Jesus as the Son of Man, which placed it in the future.

3. The contrast and the link between Jesus and John is explicated further by means of the parable of children in the marketplace (vv. 16–17), interpreted in verses 18–19 as a reference to John and Jesus. A shift in

meaning takes place between the parable and its interpretation.

In the parable it is the complaining children, not their playmates, who are in the wrong. The parable recalls the well-known occurrence of children who complain that others do not want to play with them, when in reality they themselves are the ones who do not want to join the games that are already in progress. This understanding is confirmed by the introduction: "[This generation] is like children in the marketplace who call to the others . . ." (v. 16). The situation of the complaining children illustrates what "this generation" is like, but we do not know what situation it illustrated since we do not know the parable's original context. The present context suggested by the interpretation (vv. 18–19) is secondary, as will be shown presently. Was the original point of the parable that "this generation" was like children who did not recognize that it was they who were uncooperative, who were hard of heart?

In the interpretation (vv. 18–19), the children's roles are reversed; now the other children are taken to be uncooperative; they are unwilling to play the games suggested by the complaining children. Thus verses 18–19 illustrate the people's reaction to the contrasting ways of life of John and Jesus. These verses may have originated specifically as an interpretation of the parable, but they could also have been formulated independently as a separate saying that was subsequently attached to the parable as a means of interpreting it. In any case, whether they originally constituted an independent saying or were formulated specifically to interpret the parable, verses 18–19 show the hand of the primitive church in their present formulation. The reference to Jesus as the Son of Man presupposes that he had already ascended to the right hand of God from where he was to have returned. After the understanding had developed that Jesus had ascended to heaven and had become identified with the Son of man in the sense of Daniel 7:13, New Testament Christians applied the designation *Son of Man* to him with regard to his earthly existence as well, as in the present saying.

As a product of the primitive church the saying would be remarkable; even though Jesus and John are contrasted in it, they are also presented as equivalent, which is contrary to the typical understanding of their relationship in the Gospel tradition, where John is presented as the mere forerunner of Jesus. As such, these verses probably represent an early view, if not of Jesus himself, then of his followers who were still familiar with the relationship that had actually existed between Jesus and John. We are already familiar with John as an ascetic preacher of repentance, forgiveness, and reconciliation in the face of the imminent coming of the kingdom of God; Jesus we know as someone who participated joyfully in the earthly pleasures of banquets with persons of ill repute, summarized succinctly in Luke 15:1–2, "The publicans and sinners were drawing close to him, so the Pharisees and scribes complained, saying, this man accepts sinners, and eats with them" (cf. Mark 2:15–17, //s). Our saying expresses forcefully the contrast between their ways of life, but it also expresses a certain closeness.

Nevertheless, if Jesus' way of life was reprehensible to the Pharisees and scribes, how much more might it have been to John with his professed asceticism? In such a situation of radical contrast but continuing coordination the first part of our passage, John's question about Jesus and Jesus' reply (vv. 2–6, //), becomes understandable.

We return to verses 2–6, // for clarification. As we suggested above, the present form of Matthew 11:2–67, // is a Christian formulation, for two reasons. First, John's question, "Are you the one who is coming, or must we expect another?" (v. 3), reflects the Christian understanding of him as the forerunner of Jesus, and, second, Jesus' answer is understandable only when one already knows that he was the one expected by John. We may ask, however, whether the passage is based on earlier tradition. The relationship between Jesus and John suggested in our discussion of verses 18–19 provides a setting in which the reply of Jesus can become understandable historically. In it Jesus appears to have given a justification for his controversial behavior in response to a question from John. Note especially the concluding statement, "Blessed is whoever is not scandalized by me" (v. 6, //).

Jesus' reply does not answer the present form of John's question, "Are you the one who is coming or should we expect another?" A different question is presupposed. The first part of Jesus' reply (v. 5, //) is composed of allusions and direct quotations to the following passages in Isaiah: (1) "And in that day the deaf will hear the word of Scripture; eyes that are in darkness and hazy will see; beggars will rejoice in the Lord, and those who are without hope will be filled with joy" (29:18–19). (2) "Be strong, hands that are limp and legs that are shaky; be of good cheer, you who are faint-hearted; be strong and do not fear. Behold, our Lord repays and will repay with judgment; he comes and will save us. Then the eyes of the blind will be opened. The lame will leap like a deer, and the tongue of the stutterer will be sound, for water will rise in the desert and a gully in parched land" (35:4–6). (3) "The spirit of the Lord who anointed me for this purpose is upon me. He sent me to proclaim good tidings to the poor, to heal the brokenhearted, to declare amnesty for those who have been taken captive, and sight to the blind; to announce the pleasing year of the Lord, the day of repayment; to console all those who mourn" (61:1–2).

In referring to the fulfillment of these expectations, Jesus makes no claim about his own person, merely that what Isaiah predicted was being fulfilled. Only the final statement in Jesus' reply focuses on his person: "Blessed is whoever is not scandalized by me" (v. 6). It should be noted, furthermore, that this final statement is predicated on Jesus' claim that the expectations of Isaiah were being fulfilled in the present. The first part of his reply provides the context in which the claim about himself is to be understood.

Taken in the context of the passage as a whole, it appears that Jesus justified his behavior with the claim that the kingdom of God announced by John had already arrived in the form predicted by Isaiah. John announced and prepared for the imminent coming of the kingdom of God, and according to our passage Jesus accepted that proclamation. John himself was the final eschatological figure; "The prophets and the Law are until John" (v. 13). Therefore, Jesus, who came after him, could not also be an eschatological figure; his activity had to be, so to speak, posteschatological. He was, in the words of Isaiah 61:1, the one who was anointed to receive the Spirit in order to announce good tidings to the poor: "The spirit of the Lord who anointed me for this purpose is upon me . . . to proclaim good tidings to the poor." This corresponds to the first beatitude, "Blessed are the poor, for yours is the kingdom of God" (Luke 6:20b, cf. Matt. 5:3). The first part of Isaiah 61:1 is not quoted, but, as we can see, it fits the situation of Jesus very well.

Few significant differences appear between Matthew's and Luke's versions of the traditions concerning Jesus and John. Their formulations are verbally similar, except for the introductions, which nevertheless make the same point (Matt. 11:2, //). Luke, as we have noted, does not include a parallel to Matthew 11:12–15 at this stage of his Gospel, but he quotes a somewhat different version of it in 16:16. The story was probably not an original unity but a collection of traditions. Luke's version of John sending his disciples is longer but also redundant (cf. vv. 19–20). Matthew may have abbreviated Mark in order to rid the formulation of redundancy, while Luke may have added the statement that healings had taken place just at that time (v. 21) in order to set the scene for Jesus' reply.

Conclusion. The relationship between John and Jesus as presented in the passages we have just discussed appears to have been highly paradoxical. John prepared the way for the coming of the kingdom of God, not for Jesus as another, the final, eschatological figure. John himself was the final eschatological figure before the coming of the kingdom of God. Jesus acted within the framework of John's proclamation, but, believing that the kingdom had already come, he took the next step of living out the meaning of the kingdom in word and deed. In that way he confirmed John's proclamation, emphasizing its significance with statements such as, "The prophets and the Law are until John, from then on the kingdom of God is proclaimed" (Luke 16:16, //), and "No one who was born of woman is greater than John the Baptist" (Matt. 11:11a, //). On the one hand, it is in John's activity as the final eschatological figure that Jesus found justification for his behavior, while on the other hand, it was in Jesus' activity that John's proclamation found its fulfillment. The saying "no one who was born of woman is greater than John the Baptist, but the least in the kingdom of the heavens is greater than he" (Matt. 11:11, //) expresses the paradox in a nutshell. Paradoxically, John is the greatest of all who were born of a woman *because* the least in the kingdom of God is greater than he. Without John there would be no "least in the kingdom of God," and yet, if the least in the kingdom of God were not greater than he, he would not be the greatest of anyone who was born of a woman.

This paradox is also expressed in a Christianized form in John's saying, "He who comes after me [and thus is dependent on me] is greater than me" (Matt. 3:11b, cf. //s), and even more paradoxically in the Fourth Gospel, "After me comes a person who is before me, because he is prior to me" (John 1:30). Even though these statements have highly Christianized forms, they still accurately express the paradox of the relationship between John and Jesus. By failing to maintain the paradox, New Testament Christianity did a disservice not only to John, but also to Jesus. As much as John's ultimate significance depended on the recognition (by Jesus) that the kingdom of God did come as he predicted, Jesus' proclamation depended on the recognition of John as the final eschatological figure who signaled the coming of the kingdom of God.

To focus on Jesus, to make him the final eschatological figure, is to miss his meaning. Jesus did not point to himself but to the presence of the kingdom of God and to John as the one who marked the transition from the previous age to the coming of the kingdom of God. To focus on Jesus, to see his greatness in his person alone, is to make him less, because his greatness was in his pointing to the kingdom and to John. In this context Jesus' answer to the question concerning the authority in which he acted becomes crucial: "I will ask you a single question; you answer me, and I will tell you on what authority I do these things. The baptism of John, is it from heaven or from people?" (Mark 11:29, //s). New Testament Christianity would have done well to have recognized the significance of his answer. The question concerning the authority for his activity could be answered only in the framework of the authority of John's baptism. New Testament tradition suffers from a self-destructive excess; by trying to absolutize the greatness of Jesus, it loses the tension created by the paradox of his relationship to John, which alone provides the framework within which his real significance is recognizable. By cutting down on this excess, by reestablishing John as the final eschatological figure who signaled the coming of the kingdom of God, it may be possible to recover once more the true significance and meaning of Jesus.

The meaning of Matthias Grünewald's painting reflects the situation correctly only if it is seen in tension with its inversion, Jesus pointing to John with the words, "What did you go out to see in the desert? A reed swaying in the wind? No? What then did you go out looking for? A man dressed in fine clothing? Look, persons who wear finery live in palaces! So what did you go out for? To see a prophet? Indeed, I tell you, he is more than a prophet. He is the one concerning whom it is written, 'Behold, I send my messenger before me!' In fact, no one that is born on earth is greater than John, for all the prophets and the Law prophesied until John the Baptist. If you are willing to accept this he is the expected Elijah" (Matt. 11:7–10a, 11, 13).

How did Jesus arrive at this conviction? What made him recognize John's presence as marking the transition from the time immediately before the kingdom of God to its actual coming? The confrontation between Jesus and his relatives (Mark 3:20–21, 31–35, //s), may shed some light on this question, without necessarily answering it.

C. JESUS AND HIS RELATIVES (MARK 3:20–21 31–35, //s; #116, 121)

Mark 3:20–21 and 31–35 were evidently an original unity. Verses 20–21 form an introduction to what follows in 31–35. Jesus' family—literally "those from him"; the RSV has "his friends"—try to get hold of him because they are disturbed by his behavior, which appears to them to be of someone who is not in his right mind (vv. 20–21). When they approach him through intermediaries in a house that they cannot enter, or do not want to, he rejects them and announces that not they, but those around him, are his real relatives (vv. 31–35). Mark interrupted the sequence with the story of the accusation of collusion with Satan (vv. 22–27) and the warning against blasphemy of the Holy Spirit (vv. 28–29), probably to connect it with the statement in verse 21 that Jesus was out of his mind, that is, possessed of the devil.

Matthew followed Mark by quoting parallels to both intermediary traditions (Matt. 12:22–30 and vv. 31–32), even though he already had a briefer version of the first in 9:32–34. He then added more material (vv. 33–45) before taking up the parallel to Mark 3:31–35 again in 12:46–50. Luke included no parallels to the two intermediate traditions at this stage of his Gospel, but he added another version of the first in 11:14–15, 17–23. In none of these versions (except for a single verse, Mark 3:27; Matt. 12:29) is there substantial agreement among the evangelists. All could have been quoted relatively independently of each other, lending support to the presumption that their location between Mark 3:20–21 and 31–35 was not fixed. Our interest here is not in these intermediate traditions, but in the single tradition of Mark 3:20–21, 31–35, //s.

With regard to the latter, neither Matthew nor Luke included parallels to Mark 3:20–21, apparently the story's original introduction. Matthew and Luke probably skipped the introduction because they were unable to make sense of its present position in Mark, isolated from the story that it originally introduced (vv. 31–35). However, they may also have been unwilling to include the statement that "[Jesus'] relatives went out to get hold of him, because they said he was out of his mind" (v. 21). The statement was also a problem for an early copyist who substituted "scribes and others" for the phrase "those from him," which almost certainly means "his relatives," and not merely "his friends," as the RSV translates. Indeed, according to verses 31–35 Jesus was with his friends when his relatives tried to persuade him to return home. In contrast with the intermediate traditions, all three versions of this second part of the story are very close to one another. The only variations are that Luke left out a few verses (33b–34) and inverted the order of the two clauses of verse 35 (cf. Luke 8:21). Luke also did not locate the incident parallel to Mark, who was followed by Matthew, but added it a little later in his Gospel (8:19–21).

The story agrees with a number of other facts we have already learned about Jesus, expressed succinctly in the statement that "the publicans and sinners were drawing close to him, so the Pharisees and scribes complained, saying, this man accepts sinners, and eats with them" (Mark 2:15–17, //s). It is also expressed in Jesus' own awareness that his behavior was scandalous, "Blessed is whoever is not scandalized by me" (Matt. 1:6, //). Our present passage adds Jesus' relatives to those who were—understandably—scandalized by his behavior.

The incident has become rather harmless in the history of Christianity. Jesus' relatives asked him to come with them, but he refused, indicating that those who were around him were his true relatives, "those who do the will of God" (v. 35). Jesus, it is assumed, was doing what he was supposed to do by being with publicans and sinners. The rejection of his relatives here is similar to the rebuke of his worried parents when he was left behind in Jerusalem at the age of twelve, "Why is it that you look for me? Do you not realize that I should be involved in the matters of my father?" (Luke 2:49). What escapes attention in the present passage is the irony in Jesus' justification of those around him—publicans and sinners—as his real relatives because they do the will of god. Elsewhere he gives the exact opposite reason for associating with them: "The healthy do not need the physician, but those who are ill. I did not come to call the righteous, but sinners" (Mark 2:17, //s), implying that those around him did not do the will of God.

If this is a historical incident, it was exceedingly painful for his family. Jesus, according to tradition, the oldest son in an artisan family, that is, not of the peasant or day-laborer class, first takes off to the desert with an ascetic preacher. When he returns he does not reintegrate with his family but begins to associate with all the wrong people in his hometown. In desperation—"he is out of his mind"—his relatives try to persuade him to come home but dare not enter the house where he is to be found. (Was it because they did not want to compromise themselves because the house, filled with Jesus' "publican and sinner" friends, was ritually impure?) They send word to him by intermediaries, but his reply is a harsh rejection, reaffirming his scandalous behavior. The scene is typical; many young men probably behaved in a similar way before Jesus, and many more certainly did so after him. Jesus, it appears, was a black sheep. According to one evangelist, his mother stayed with him to the end (cf. John 19:25–27), but his brothers resented him (cf. John 7:3–5).

According to tradition, Jesus gave at least three reasons for his behavior. In the present passage the explanation is that those around him were the ones who did the will of God (Mark 3:35, //s). Historically, it is the least probable, since the persons with whom he associated are typically presented as sinners, that is, as persons who did not do the will of God. Primitive Christianity, however, idealized the scene to represent Jesus' choice to do the will of God, even at the expense of family ties. He directed his followers to do the same: "He who loves father and mother more than me is not worthy of me" (Matt. 10:3, cf., 11).

A second reason Jesus gave for his behavior was that it was not the healthy who needed a physician but those who were ill, and that he did not come for the sake of the righteous but for sinners (Mark 2:17, //s). This answer takes into account that those with whom he associated did not do the will of God and agrees with the general picture of Jesus according to the Gospel tradition. It is also not in disagreement with the third reason, although the emphasis is different.

The third reason is the one we already know from his reply to John's question: the kingdom of God has already arrived and therefore no one should be scandalized by his behavior (Matt. 11:5, //). It is certainly the boldest justification. The first merely claims that this associates obey the will of God; the second expresses Jesus' willingness to associate with the religious and moral outcasts of society; but the third grounds his behavior in the activity of God himself, whose kingdom he believed had already arrived. The boldness of this claim was that his behavior, scandalous as it may have been, was grounded in the will of God. This is similar to Jesus' claim that the authority for his activity was the same as that of John, as we have seen above (Mark 11:27–33, //s).

We cannot be sure which, if any, of these justifications go back to Jesus himself, or whether he may not have given all of them in some form or other on various occasions. The first certainly appears historically improbable and may be a product of New Testament Christianity.

Another crucial question, arising particularly in connection with the third justification, is whether Jesus' behavior was actually motivated by his conviction that the kingdom of God had come or whether he merely developed that view as an argument to justify his scandalous behavior. We do not have sufficient information to answer this question either. We do know, however, that Christianity was rooted in the understanding that Jesus acted in the name of God. In whatever way his behavior may have been motivated, it was in interpreting it within the framework of John's proclamation of the kingdom of God that Christianity was rooted, in the paradox of his scandalous behavior motivated by the coming of God's kingdom. In the final analysis it may not really matter whether Jesus' behavior was motivated by his belief that the kingdom of God had been ushered in by the activity of John the Baptist or whether he merely developed that conviction to justify his scandalous behavior. What does matter is that the placement of his association with religious and social outcasts within the framework of the coming of the kingdom of God became one of the crucial marks of those who came to believe in him.

Conclusion. At some stage of his life Jesus evidently became part of the movement of the ascetic prophet, John the Baptist, whom he followed to the desert area around the lower Jordan where he was baptized. He evidently did not remain in the company of John as one of his disciples but returned to Galilee where we encounter him in the Gospel stories. However, even after he had left the circle of John's followers, he still maintained his high regard for his former teacher, affirming John's ascetic mode of existence against criticism (Matt. 11:7–9, //). He also expressed the conviction that John superseded all other prophets and that John was the returning Elijah who marked the transition of the ages from the time before the kingdom of God to the time of its coming (Matt. 11:9–14, //).

Jesus himself, however, entered into a way of life diametrically opposed to that of John, as expressed in the saying with which the parable of the children in the marketplace is interpreted (Matt. 11:16–19, //). What is most remarkable about this saying is that it expresses a fundamental continuity between the activity of John and Jesus, notwithstanding the fact that John withdrew as an ascetic into the desert, away from sinful humanity, in anticipation of the awesome dawning of the kingdom of God, whereas Jesus entered into joyful table fellowship with the representatives of the very same sinful humanity from which John withdrew.

Jesus' behavior was scandalous. He himself accepted that it was so in his reply to John's question, "Blessed is whoever is not scandalized by me" (Matt. 11:6, //). Concrete evidence of his outrageous behavior is provided by the confrontation between him and his family in their attempt to persuade him to come home with them, especially by his reaction to their request (Mark 3:20–21, 32–35, //s). The painful embarrassment to which Jesus subjected his relatives is masked only by the idealizing of the scene in the Christian tradition.

We do not know what motivated Jesus' scandalous behavior. It is a type of behavior, often repeated, that in one sense needs no explanation; many young people from good families have behaved in similar ways. What is remarkable is that from the behavior of Jesus a world religion was born. A crucial factor in its formative influence appears to have been Jesus' interpretation of his activity as rooted in John the Baptist's preaching of the imminent coming of the kingdom of God. This explanation gave his own actions a deeply religious connotation, but it does not explain everything.

A crucial incident in the life of Jesus according to the synoptics is the confession of Peter followed by the first prediction of the passion (Mark 8:27–30, //s). In the Gospels it is decisive for an understanding of who Jesus was. The passage is also important because it prepares for Jesus' passion and execution as a messianic pretender.

CHAPTER 3

Peter's Confession and the Predictions of the Passion
(Mark 8:27–33; 9:30–32; 10:32–34; cf. 6:14–16, //s)

Mark 8:27–33 (#158–59) has two distinguishable but nevertheless closely related parts: the so-called confession of Peter (vv. 27–30) and the first prediction of the passion (vv. 31–33). What is striking about the first part is that while Jesus himself prompts Peter to make the declaration, he commands the disciples to keep its contents secret. Two questions arise: what does *messiah* mean in Peter's declaration, and why did Jesus demand silence of his disciples?

We have strong indications that at least some of Jesus' followers had political aspirations. According to Luke 24:21 the two disciples who spoke to the unrecognized Jesus on the way to Emmaus told him that they had hoped that "he is the one who was to redeem Israel." The meaning of this is stated more explicitly by the disciples who ask Christ as he is about to ascend into heaven, "Are you now going to reestablish the kingdom of Israel?" (Acts 1:6). The whole of Acts, concluding with Paul's arrival in Rome, is, in a sense, a negative reply to that question. As Jesus states in his reply, "But you will receive strength with the coming of the Holy Spirit over you, and you will be my witnesses in Jerusalem, and in all of Judea and Samaria, and to the ends of the earth" (Acts 1:8). It is significant that Luke, who in this way so strongly opposed the conception of a political messiahship of Jesus, nevertheless presented his disciples as having held that view. The very fact that Jesus became known as the messiah in the setting of Jewish Palestine, prior to the subsequent Christian reinterpretation of the title, is in itself an indication that political expectations may

54

have been involved. And it was, indeed, on the charge of being a messianic pretender that Jesus was executed by the Romans.

In Mark 8:31–33, however, Jesus' messiahship is interpreted in the sense of his suffering as the Son of Man. But it should be noted that this interpretation is formulated almost as a challenge to the disciples: "And turning around and looking at the disciples he rebuked Peter and said, 'Go away from me, Satan; you do not think of the things of God, but of humans.' " According to Mark 9:32, even after the second prediction of the passion the disciples did not understand what Jesus meant. What Peter intended with the declaration appears not to be the same as what Jesus had in mind. This problem is fundamental to the passage, but in order to solve it we must first try to understand how the passage was composed. A good place to start is to answer the second question above, why Jesus commanded his disciples to remain silent about his messiahship.

A. THE SO-CALLED MESSIANIC SECRET IN MARK

Jesus repeats the command to remain silent in Mark 9:9, after his transfiguration on the mountain (vv. 2–8, #161). In this case, however, he demands that the secret be kept only until "the Son of Man rose from the dead." In both cases the identification of Jesus, as messiah in 8:29 and as Son of God in 9:7, is followed by a command to secrecy. This same motif occurs in connection with the demons who already know the identity of Jesus. They too are commanded by Jesus to remain silent (1:24–25, 34, cf. 5:7). Similarly, Jesus repeatedly commands silence after performing a miracle (1:44; 5:43; 7:36), a command, however, that is not obeyed (cf. 1:45; 7:36). As a result Jesus' renown grows despite his own intentions (1:28; 2:12; 7:36).

This secrecy motif is present in Matthew and Luke only in parallels to Mark. It has thus been argued with good reason that the motif is specifically Markan, and that its purpose was to present the messiahship of Jesus as a secret to be revealed only after his resurrection (9:9). Where his renown did grow it was contrary to his own intentions.

Mark 9:9 is not an integral part of the story to which it refers but is attached to it. As an expression of the so-called messianic secret motif it could have been added by Mark himself. The same is true for 8:30. If the story of the actual confession of Peter (vv. 27–30) is taken by itself as a separate story, verse 30 seems to be very loosely attached at the end. If, on the other hand, the more extended passage (verses 27–33) is taken as a unity, verse 30 becomes more integral to the story but nevertheless still fits very loosely in its context. In both cases the verse can be removed without disturbing the continuity. Verse 31 could follow after verse 29 as smoothly as it does after the present verse 30.

It thus appears that Mark 8:30 may also be an expression of the so-called messianic secret motif, introduced by Mark himself into our passage (8:27–33). There are two ways in which Mark could have done this.

He could simply have added it to an existing story, either at the end of verses 27–29 or in between verses 29 and 31. The other possibility is that 8:27–33 is a composition by Mark himself in which he united a variety of traditions and themes, including the secrecy motif, to produce a new compositional unity. That does not have to mean that his choices were arbitrary. As a Gospel writer he was not merely a collector of tradition but also an interpreter of it.

B. THE PARALLEL IN MARK 6:14–16 (#143)

An indication that 8:27–33 is composite and not a single tradition is the presence in verse 28 of material that occurs elsewhere in the gospel in a different context, that is, in 6:14–16. Several clues indicate that 6:14–16 is itself composite. Verse 16a, "And hearing, Herod said," repeats what is written in verse 14a, "And King Herod heard." What appears to have happened in the composition of this passage is that a phrase from one tradition, "For his name became known" (v. 14b), was expounded by means of another tradition that indicated the variety of ways in which Jesus had become known (vv. 14c–15). This exposition, however, interrupted the original continuity of verses 14ab and 16b, "And King Herod heard, for his name became known, and he said, he whom I beheaded, John, was resurrected." This interruption made it necessary to repeat what had already been said in verse 14a in the new formulation of verse 16a. Herod's response then leads to the tradition of the death of the Baptist (6:17–29), which his statement presupposes.

The statements concerning what the people thought about Jesus in Mark 6:14c–15 and in 8:28 appear to have been drawn from the same tradition. That tradition provided one of the elements in Mark's composition of 8:27–22.

Matthew and Luke both correct Mark's "king" in 6:14 with "tetrarch." Matthew furthermore eliminates the additional conceptions of who Jesus was from the tradition of Mark 6:14c–15, leaving only the identification of Jesus with the resurrected Baptist as a proposal of Herod's servants. He gives no indication what Herod himself thought. Luke retains all the references but reformulates the passage stylistically (under the influence of another version of the tradition?). He too does not have Herod state that Jesus was the resurrected Baptist, merely that Herod wondered who Jesus could have been.

C. THE PREDICTIONS OF THE PASSION

A further indication that Mark 8:27–33 is composite is the use that Mark made in it of the prediction of the passion (8:31), which is repeated in 9:31 (#164) and 10:33–34 (#262). A comparison between the three predictions reveals 9:31 to be the briefest. It may reflect an original Aramaic paradoxical saying, "The Son of Man is handed over to sons of men." "Son of Man" is a title for Jesus expressing his heavenly dignity, and "sons of men" is a reference to mere humans. The brief formula of 9:31 was apparently expanded into a summary of Mark's own passion narrative in 10:33–34. Mark 8:31 was similarly expanded, but not nearly to the same degree as 10:33–34.

Peter, in reacting to Jesus' prediction (8:32), ignored Jesus' mention of the resurrection. It was obviously the passion to which he objected. His reaction to the resurrection should probably be taken in the sense of 9:10: the disciples did not understand what Jesus meant with "rising from the dead." The focus on the passion alone in Peter's reaction to Jesus prediction and the focus on the resurrection in 9:10 reveal that verse 31 was formulated with not only the present passage in mind; it presented the events of the passion and resurrection as a global unity. The disciples, however, reacted separately to the passion and to the resurrection. Their reaction to the passion was an unqualified rejection (v. 31); to the resurrection, incomprehension (9:10). Only Mark 9:32 is a more general reaction to the entire statement of Jesus.

The predictions of the passion were drawn from the very event that they predicted. This can be seen clearly in the details with which they have been expanded, especially in 10:33–34. The Aramaic wordplay on which the prophecies were based did not predict but merely expressed the paradox that the Son of Man should fall so completely into the hands of (the sons of) men. Mark skillfully used the formulations of the predictions in their present form to clarify that Jesus' forthcoming passion was not unanticipated but was the purpose for which he went up to Jerusalem. They function as decisive interpretive tools to leave the reader with little doubt, when reaching the final part of the Gospel, that the passion was the culmination of Jesus' activity. The first prediction in 8:32 begins the process of interpreting Peter's recognition of Jesus as the messiah in terms of the passion that it anticipates.

D. THE COMPOSITION OF MARK 8:27–33

Our investigation has revealed so far that in formulating 8:27–33 Mark used at least two independent traditions (vv. 28 and 31), and that he himself may have formulated verse 30 as an expression of the messianic secret motif. We now note that the way he structured the first part of the passage (vv. 27–30) is similar in some ways to 9:2–9, the story of the transfiguration. In both cases Jesus' identity is revealed in the circle of his intimate followers, and this revelation is followed by the command to secrecy. Peter's declaration that Jesus is the messiah (8:29) is paralleled by the divine voice declaring that he is his beloved son (9:7). This parallelism in the structure expresses a certain parallelism in the meanings of the two passages as well. Both contain statements about Jesus' identity—that he is the messiah (8:29), the Son of God (9:7)—combined in a single formulation in the high priest's question in the trial before the **Sanhedrin**, "Are you the messiah, the son of the blessed one?" (Mark 14:61, //). Mark 8:27–30 and 9:2–9 are two different statements of what is in fact a single identification of Jesus. To be the messiah is to be the Son of God and vice versa, although the latter term is probably understood to express this single conception at a deeper level.

It thus appears that all three passages (Mark 8:27–33; 9:2–10; and 14:61) are related in that they all answer, from Mark's point of view, the question of who Jesus was. However, whereas Jesus commanded his disciples in 8:30 and 9:9 not to reveal this truth—according to 9:9 "not until the Son of Man rose from the dead"—he himself allowed it to become public at his trial before the Sanhedrin. It may also be significant that it is already at his death, not after his resurrection, that the centurion recognizes that he is "indeed a son of God" (15:39).

If we also include 8:31–33 in our deliberations, another structural similarity between 8:27–33 and Jesus' declaration before the Sanhedrin is revealed. In both cases the declaration that Jesus is the messiah (the Son of God) is followed by an interpretation—in 8:31 by the prediction of Jesus' suffering and resurrection, and in 14:62 by messianic passages from Scripture. These interpretations are progressive. The interpretation of 8:31 in terms of Jesus' suffering is not repeated in 14:62 because, as 14:41 indicates, Jesus had already entered into the suffering predicted in 8:31. Thus in 14:62 the focus is on the future of the resurrection, not on the passion as in 8:31.

After the second prediction of the passion (9:31), Mark states that even though the disciples did not understand what Jesus meant, they were afraid to ask him about it (v. 32). And when, after the transfiguration, Jesus commanded them to keep secret what they saw until the resurrection had taken place (9:9), they wondered what Jesus meant by "rising from the dead" (v. 10). Here in 8:31–33 their lack of understanding is even more radical. Peter dares to contradict Jesus, bringing Jesus' harsh rebuke upon himself (v. 33). That Jesus turned around to face the rest of the disciples evidently indicates that the rebuke was directed to them as well.

All of this taken together suggests that, notwithstanding the formulation of 9:9, the messianic secret motif did not concern specifically the resurrection of Jesus but expressed the idea that his messiahship had to be kept secret because its meaning could not be grasped outside the context of the passion and resurrection of Jesus. Not even his disciples, to whom he tried to communicate this meaning by means of the predictions of the passion, were able to understand it until the resurrection had taken place. (We can only presume this final understanding because Mark nowhere reports it.) It seems clear that Mark was aware that the disciples' conception of Jesus' messiahship was contrary to the subsequent Christian conception to which Mark himself adhered, and for which the passion and resurrection were of central importance.

Jesus' interpretation of the meaning of his messiahship to his uncomprehending disciples in terms of his death and resurrection is also the theme of the post-resurrection tradition of Luke 24:13–21, 25–27 (#355). When the unrecognized Jesus pretends ignorance of the events about which the two disciples were conversing they reply, "Concerning Jesus of Nazareth, a prophet powerful in deed and word before God and all the people; how our chief priests and leaders handed him over to be condemned to death, and crucified him. We hoped that he was the one who was to redeem Israel, but now it is with all of this already the third day since those things happened" (vv. 19–21). Jesus replied to this by rebuking them for their inability to understand. " 'Oh, how ignorant you are and unwilling to believe everything that was said by the prophets. Was it not necessary that the messiah should die and so enter into his glory?' And beginning from Moses and all the prophets he interpreted to them from all the Scriptures the facts concerning himself" (vv. 26–27). The reference to the women at the grave in vv. 22–24 is not an original part of this tradition. It is obviously an interpolation from the resurrection tradition, one that leaves the despair of the two disciples incomprehensible. As in Mark 8:27–33, so also in this passage Jesus points out that not only is his passion not contrary to his messiahship, but that it is essential for an understanding of it. We will come back to this Lukan passage later in our study. For the moment it is sufficient to note the remarkable degree to which it reflects the same issues as Mark 8:27–33—the problem of the passion of Jesus and the resolution of that problem by interpreting it as essential to an understanding of his messiahship. The only real difference is that in Mark 8:27–33 the explanation is projected back into the life of Jesus before his crucifixion. Matthew goes a step further by denying that at any time the disciples failed to understand the explanation given by Jesus, thus projecting their understanding of the mission of Jesus back to the time before the crucifixion.

E. THE MEANING OF THE PASSAGE

The present passage marks an important transition in Mark's Gospel from vague rumors concerning who Jesus might have been to the true understanding of him as the messiah, interpreted in terms of his forthcoming passion and resurrection. Mark gives compositional expression to this, on the one hand, by repeating the people's speculations concerning his identity (v. 28, cf. 6:14c–15), followed by the declaration that Jesus is the messiah (v. 29), thus posing the declaration of his true identity against the vague rumors of the first part of the Gospel, and, on the other hand, by having Jesus interpret his messiahship by means of the prediction of the passion (v. 31). Continuity with the passion is maintained throughout the second part of the Gospel by Jesus twice repeating the prediction in the narrative that follows (9:31 and 10:33–34). He then calls for the final, paradoxical act to begin when he declares, "The hour has come; behold, the Son of Man is handed over into the hands of sinners" (14:41).

By juxtaposing the first prediction of the passion with Peter's confession of Jesus as the messiah, Mark has Jesus pose the correct understanding of his messiahship against the disciples' inability to understand it. From now on the Gospel no longer concerns the vague rumors but proceeds on the basis of an understanding of him as the messiah who was to suffer and be resurrected. This understanding is reinforced by the declaration of him as the Son of God in the transfiguration on the mountain (9:2–8).

The most crucial event in the passage is the declaration that Jesus is the messiah. Because of its ambiguity it is not the most decisive, but it is precisely this ambiguity that makes it so crucial. It marks an important transition in the Gospel but does not by itself clarify who Jesus is. That is why the disciples are commanded to keep it secret. It could not be understood correctly until it was possible to interpret it within the context of the passion and resurrection. Jesus tried to dissolve the ambiguity by interpreting it to the intimate circle of disciples by means of the first prediction of the passion, but they did not understand him. That is what is decisive.

Here Jesus interprets to the intimate circle of disciples, excluding all who do not belong to that circle, the meaning of his messiahship: he is a messiah who must die and rise again. Mark prepares his readers for this disclosure with the statement in 4:11b–c: "To you the mystery of the kingdom of God is revealed [literally "given"]; to those outside everything comes in parables." Up to this point the Gospel does not provide any such revelation to the disciples, but that is clearly what takes place here. Note the comment that follows the prediction of the passion in the present passage, "And he spoke the word openly." Christian readers who know the entire Gospel from beginning to end are at a certain disadvantage with regard to the flow of the narrative. When Jesus tells his disciples, "To you the mystery of the kingdom of God is revealed; to those outside everything comes in parables," we are not left in suspense because we already know everything, and so we miss the suspense with which Mark wants to capture the attention of his readers. Mark's Gospel is not a theology in narrative form, which can then be reinterpreted systematically; its meaning is in the narrative itself, not in a purported theology underlying it. The idea of a theology does not explain, but rather obscures, the events in Mark. It may be possible to understand Mark's Gospel as a narrative theology if one takes theology, in Plato's sense, as a myth, but in that case narrative, in the form of a myth, explains the meaning of theology, and not the other way around, making the term *narrative theology* completely redundant.

After clarifying the meaning of his messiahship Jesus converses frankly in the intimate circle of his disciples about the "mystery" of the kingdom of God that would remain concealed from those outside until the passion and resurrection had taken place. The mystery that was revealed to the disciples (cf. 4:11), but that they did not understand (cf. 4:13), was that Jesus was the messiah (8:29) in the sense of his passion and resurrection (v. 31). In New Testament times the most common meaning of *mystery* as used by Jesus in 4:11 was the dying and rising deity of the **mystery religions**. That is the meaning expressed when Jesus commands the disciples to keep secret the knowledge revealed in the interpretation of Peter's confession by means of the prediction of the passion. The rest of the Gospel is an exposition of that mystery. According to Mark, only Jesus, the cult deity and initiator into the mystery, understood this before (and during) the passion—until the centurion recognized it when he saw the way Jesus died (15:39).

Mark states clearly that Peter as spokesman for the disciples did not understand *messiah* in the sense intended by Jesus, and Mark makes good use of Peter's inability to understand Jesus to bring out the true meaning of his messiahship. The disciples had come to recognize that Jesus was the messiah (8:29) and were in that regard a clear step ahead of the people (v. 28), but they too could not understand the secret of its meaning (vv. 32–33) until after the crucifixion and resurrection, that is, after they had actually experienced the mystery of the kingdom of God.

The Gospel of Mark, it appears, is not a report of events in the life of Jesus that lead up to his death, but a cultic myth in which the mystery of the kingdom of God is gradually disclosed, beginning with Peter's confession and the interpretation of it by means of the first prediction of the passion, and then leading deeper into it with the second and third predictions until Jesus finally announces that the actual mystery was about to begin in 14:41, "The hour has come, behold the Son of Man is handed over into the hands of sinners."

The disciples' ignorance should not be taken in the sense of a mere report of their inability to understand Jesus, although that too is involved. In the sense of Mark's Gospel as a cultic myth the disciples represent the initiates who stand in uncomprehending awe before the mystery that is being disclosed, in contrast with those outside with their loose speculations, and probably also in contrast with the centurion who remains a spectator, notwithstanding the fact that it is he who first recognizes that Jesus is "truly a son of God" (15:39). It now also becomes clear why the Gospel ends as it does, why it has to end that way, with the young man's statement, "Say to the disciples and to Peter, 'He proceeds ahead of you to Galilee. There you will see him, as he told you,' " and with the women's awed flight from the grave, "They fled from the tomb because they were trembling, beside themselves. And they said nothing to anyone, because they were afraid" (16:8). The Gospel prepares for the manifestation of the presence of the risen Lord in the worshiping community.

F. THE MATTHEAN AND LUKAN PARALLELS

Matthew and Luke follow Mark rather closely in the entire passage, except that Matthew adds the section where Peter receives the keys of the kingdom (16:17–19), which is a postresurrection tradition establishing Peter as the primary authority in the church (cf. 1 Cor. 15:5). Luke omits both Peter's rejection of Jesus' explanation and Jesus reprimanding him for doing so (Mark 8:32–33). The only significant agreement between Matthew and Luke against Mark is that they both have "on the third day he will be raised," against Mark's "after three days he will rise" (Mark 8:31, //s). This does not suggest a separate tradition for the present passage but is probably a correction in accord with the tradition that Jesus was resurrected, not after three days, but on the third day. Matthew has the same disagreement with Mark in the parallel to the second passion prediction (Mark 9:31, //s), where Luke has no reference to the resurrection at all. Matthew and Luke also agree against Mark on the day of the resurrection, in their parallels to the third prediction (Mark 10:33–34).

It is worth noting that in the parallel to the third prediction Luke includes the statement that Jesus was spat upon (18:32, cf. Mark 10:34), although in his own passion narrative no reference is made to it (22:63–65, cf. Mark 14:65). This probably indicates his dependence on Mark for the formulation in 18:32. Matthew, on the other hand, who does include the reference to Jesus being spat upon in his passion narrative (26:67), for some reason leaves it out here (cf. 20:19).

Matthew furthermore omits the reference to the disciples' inability to understand Jesus (Mark 9:32), as we have seen, a typical feature of his Gospel (cf. Mark 4:11, //s). The statement that the disciples "were greatly grieved" after Jesus made the second prediction of the passion (17:23), suggests that they became painfully aware of the true nature of his messiahship. The understanding of Jesus' messiahship in terms of his passion, which Mark reserves for Jesus alone, is extended by Matthew to include the disciples as well. Luke, on the other hand, expands the statement of the disciples' inability to understand Jesus in the parallel to Mark 9:32, "They did not understand this word; it was concealed from them, so that they did not comprehend it" (Luke 9:45). He adds a similar statement after the third prediction (18:34). Apart from these differences and other minor changes, Matthew and Luke follow Mark rather closely in these passages.

Matthew and Luke did not recognize Mark's Gospel as a cultic myth, and certainly they did not intend their Gospels as cultic myths in that sense. Therefore they could not end their Gospels where Mark did; without the resurrection appearances their Gospels would have been incomplete. This probably also contributed to Matthew's elimination of all the references to the disciples' inability to understand. In the sense of his Gospel their ignorance placed them in a too negative light. For Matthew they represented the beginning of an understanding Christian community. In the Gospels of Matthew and Luke a transition was made from the present reality of the resurrected Jesus in the cult of the worshiping community to an interest in the past history of Jesus.

Conclusion. Mark 8:27–33 is a well-constructed dialogue between Jesus and his disciples in which Mark used both traditional material and his own formulations to present the correct understanding of the messiahship of Jesus in contrast with the people's speculations. In this the disciples filled an intermediary role, recognizing Jesus as the messiah without understanding what it meant.

Notwithstanding Jesus' attempts at clarification, the disciples did not recognize that his messiahship could be grasped only within the framework of his passion and resurrection until these events had actually taken place. The same understanding was expressed in the tradition of the Emmaus disciples in Luke 24:13–21, 25–28. The difference is that in Mark 8:27–33 this understanding is projected back into the life of Jesus as the "mystery" of the kingdom of God into which Jesus tried to initiate his disciples, but which no one except he himself understood. The disciples knew what the mystery was—that Jesus was the messiah—but they did not understand its meaning as a mystery. Matthew went a step further by eliminating all references to the disciples' inability to understand Jesus, presenting them as having become painfully aware of the nature of his messiahship after the second prediction of the passion (17:23).

With regard to the question of who Jesus was, our passage reveals that Mark was aware that the understanding of Jesus' messiahship in terms of his passion and resurrection did not arise among his followers until after these events had occurred. We have three stages in the development of this understanding: (1) The tradition of Luke 24 presents it as an interpretation that Jesus gave after his resurrection to the two disillusioned disciples on the way to Emmaus; (2) Mark projects the understanding back into the life of Jesus as an interpretation that he had given to the intimate circle of his disciples but that they did not grasp; (3) Matthew goes a step further by presenting the disciples as having come to the correct understanding of the messiahship of Jesus.

The significance of this for understanding Jesus historically is that we will have to exclude from our considerations the conception of his messiahship in terms of his passion and resurrection. This understanding of his messiahship was evidently a product of his disciples' attempt to cope with the events of his passion and death and to interpret his messiahship in that light. In the final part of this study, however, we will show how that understanding arose in the postcrucifixion community of his followers. What is important to note here is that attempts to interpret Jesus' messiahship in the light of his passion and death presuppose that he was understood as the messiah in some sense already before his passion. The most obvious prepassion conception of his messiahship would have been as a political pretender. The resistance of the disciples to the interpretation of Jesus' messiahship in terms of his passion lends support to the view that they thought of him in such political terms.

CHAPTER 4

The Trial Before the Sanhedrin
(Mark 14:53–65, //s; #332)

In one sense the trial of Jesus before the Sanhedrin is the high point of the Gospel tradition because this is where Jesus solemnly declares, under questioning by his adversaries, that he is the messiah, the Son of God (Mark 14:61–62, //s). It is this declaration that prompts his condemnation to death (v. 64, //) and his subsequent execution as king of the Jews (15:26, //s).

A. THE GOSPELS AND HISTORICAL INQUIRY

From the point of view of the Gospels we have no reason to question whether this is the way things happened. Mark and Matthew especially are not products of historical investigation but rather express the significance of Jesus as he is presented in the traditions on which they are based. Only in Luke do we find anything approaching a critical evaluation of these traditions with regard to their reliability, as he indicates in the beginning of his Gospel: "It occurred also to me to investigate carefully these things, starting from the beginning, and to write to you, honorable Theophilus" (1:3). Luke's Gospel does indeed give evidence of critical evaluation. Nevertheless, his primary intention also was not to present a critical account, but to write so that the reader "may know the truth concerning the matters reported" (v. 4). Although Luke does provide alternative versions for much of what is reported in Mark, which may be attributed at least in part to his critical investigations, Luke clearly affirms the essential facts of the Markan story. Luke's critical revisions are more concerned with details than the story itself. The situation is similar in Matthew.

When raising critical historical questions we should be aware that we are engaging in an enterprise very different from that of the Gospel writers. Our basic interest is to trace the history of the traditions that were used by the evangelists in the writing of their Gospels. We will find that things did not always take place historically as the Gospels report them, which is already suggested by the fact that the Gospels themselves frequently report the same event differently. This does not necessarily detract from their value, because for them the reported events had symbolic significance. Their purpose was to bring out that significance, to which the question of historical accuracy was subservient. Our concern for the history behind the Gospel accounts, however, forces us to make primary what is a subservient concern in the Gospels. It should be remembered, therefore, that we are not competing with the Gospels. The results of our inquiry do not challenge the presentation of the significance of Jesus for faith in the Gospels. The reader of the Gospels should attend to their presentations of Jesus, not to a Jesus behind the Gospels as presented by historical investigation. Jesus has meaning for faith as he is presented in the Gospels. Our concern here, however, is to clarify the history behind the Gospels. If this is properly understood it may also contribute to a better understanding of the distinctive meaning of Jesus in the Gospels.

The difference between a historical-critical approach and the approach of the Gospels becomes clear when one considers the crucial question, what constituted the blasphemy for which Jesus was convicted by the Sanhedrin? From a historical point of view, nothing Jesus said could have been considered blasphemy in a Jewish high court. From the point of view of Mark and Matthew, however, this poses no problem; for them the question of Jesus' purported blasphemy was conceived quite generally, not in the precise sense of a Jewish court. In these two Gospels the high priest and the rest of the Sanhedrin convicted Jesus for claiming to be the very person that he was, the Son of God. The question of the specific content of the blasphemy was of so little consequence to Mark and Matthew as to be irrelevant. Anything Jesus could have said as a declaration of his identity—the affirmation that he was indeed the messiah, the Son of God (Mark 14:61e–62a, //), as well as the reference to his sitting as the Son of Man at the right hand of God and his subsequent coming on the clouds of heaven (14:62b, //)—constituted grounds for his condemnation by an unbelieving high priest and Sanhedrin.

The situation had already changed in Luke. He found it necessary to distinguish between, on the one hand, the question whether Jesus was the messiah, coupled with the reference to him as the Son of Man seated at the right hand of God (v. 69), and, on the other, Jesus' affirmation that he was indeed the Son of God (v. 70). The first question leads directly to the second, but in Luke it is the latter that constituted the grounds for condemnation: "We ourselves have heard it from his mouth" (v. 71). Note, however, that Luke avoids any reference to blasphemy.

According to Luke, Jesus was condemned because he claimed to have been the Son of God. What type of crime was that, historically speaking? And what do Mark and Matthew have in mind when they report that Jesus was found guilty of blasphemy? Historically, that is the greatest difficulty with the account because everything we know of Judaism at that time suggests that Jesus said nothing that could have been considered blasphemy by the Sanhedrin. Furthermore, at a number of points the procedure described, particularly in Mark and Matthew, violates the rules for a Sanhedrin trial according to Jewish tradition. At this point it would be useful to review what we know about the rules by which a Sanhedrin trial should have operated in the time of Jesus.

B. THE TRIAL AND THE TRACTATE *SANHEDRIN*

We do not have written records from Jesus' time indicating the procedures to be followed in a Sanhedrin trial, but the subsequent recording of the oral traditions in the **Mishnah** provides valuable information. The gathering and editing of these rules were done by Jehuda the Patriarch, referred to in Jewish writings simply as Rabbi, who worked in Sepphoris in Galilee and lived from A.D. 135–220. Since the rules were written down later we cannot be sure of the applicability of each one of them in the time of Jesus, but generally speaking we may assume that the rules recorded by Jehuda did apply at that time. Confirmation is provided in a number of cases by comparing the Lukan version of the trial of Jesus with those of Mark and Matthew.

One solution of the procedural inconsistencies is frequently offered but should be rejected at the outset: that the Sanhedrin was so intent on condemning Jesus that they disregarded their own rules. The Jewish leadership was evidently out to get Jesus, but we may take it as certain that they would have done so on the basis of their own legal codes, not in violation of them. Luke's alternate presentation of certain details in agreement with the rules described in the Mishnah suggests strongly that we look for another solution.

Especially in capital cases the Sanhedrin was intent on providing the best possible chance of acquittal. The following points from the tractate *Sanhedrin* 4:1, 5 and 5:2 are worth noting:

1. Noncapital cases were decided by three judges, capital cases by twenty-three.
2. In noncapital cases arguments could begin with reasons for either acquittal or conviction, but capital cases had to begin with reasons for acquittal.
3. In noncapital cases a verdict of either acquittal or conviction could be reached by a majority of one, but in capital cases only a verdict of

acquittal could be reached by a majority of one. A verdict of conviction had to be reached by a majority of two.

4. In noncapital cases a verdict could be reversed from conviction to acquittal or from acquittal to conviction, but in capital cases a reversal could be made only from conviction to acquittal, not from acquittal to conviction.

5. In noncapital cases everyone could argue in favor of either acquittal or conviction, but in capital cases all could argue for acquittal but not in favor of conviction.

6. In noncapital cases a judge who had argued in favor of conviction could change his mind and argue in favor of acquittal, and vice versa, but in a capital case a change of argument could take place only in favor of acquittal.

7. In noncapital cases the trial was held in the daytime and the verdict could be reached at night, but in capital cases the trial had to be held in the daytime and the verdict also reached in the daytime.

8. In noncapital cases either verdict could be reached on the same day, but in capital cases only a verdict of acquittal could be reached on the same day. A verdict of conviction could not be reached until the next day.

9. In noncapital cases a witness could atone for a wrongful conviction by payment of money, but in capital cases a witness was answerable for the blood of a person wrongfully convicted.

10. In all cases, if witnesses contradicted each other their evidence became invalid.

To these we may add the following:

11. The punishment for blasphemy was stoning (Sanh. 7:4).

12. The rules for a conviction for blasphemy were very stringent. A person could not be found guilty unless he or she had actually pronounced the divine name itself. During the trial a substitute for the name of God was used in giving witness, but sentence could not be pronounced on the basis of the substitute name. All visitors were asked to leave the place of assembly, and the chief witness was then asked to say the precise words that had been pronounced by the accused, using the divine name itself. The other witnesses were then asked to confirm whether this was what the accused had said. The verdict was then reached on the basis of that witness. (Sanh. 7:5).

13. Even when a person was taken away to be stoned everything had to be done to ensure the possibility of a stay of execution if last-minute evidence in favor of the accused turned up. One person stood with a towel at the door of the court, and another, mounted on a horse, waited as far on the way to the place of execution as possible, but so that he could still see the person at the door. If someone in the court said that he or she still had something to argue in favor of acquittal, the man at the door had to wave the towel and the man on the horse

then rushed to stay the execution. Even if the convicted person claimed to have something to add to the evidence, she or he had to be brought back and the trial had to resume. This procedure could occur up to five times. Even as the condemned was led forth to be stoned, a herald had to cry out, announcing what the offense had been, who the witnesses were, and to request that if someone knew anything that would favor acquittal, such a one should come forward and plead the case of the convicted person (Sanh. 6:1).

From all of this it is clear that the Sanhedrin considered the taking of a life with the utmost seriousness, even if it was in the execution of justice. Their caution was expressed in the statement that follows an interpretation of the slaying of Abel by Cain. The tractate Sanhedrin observes that only a single person was created in the world (and all others in that one's image) in order to teach that if someone "caused a single soul to perish from Israel, Scripture imputes it to him as though he had caused a whole world to perish," and, inversely, if someone "saves [the life of] a single soul from Israel, Scripture imputes it to him as though he had saved . . . a whole world" (Sanh. 4:5, cf. point 9 above. Quoted from The Mishnah, ed. Herbert Danby [London: Oxford University Press, 1933; reprint 1958], p. 388).

C. LUKE AND THE TRACTATE SANHEDRIN

If we now compare the accounts of the trial in Mark and Matthew with that of Luke we find that Luke's account agrees with every Sanhedrin rule that is violated in the Markan account.

1. Whereas Mark records that the trial took place at night (Mark 15:1), Luke places it the following morning (cf. Luke 22:66). This makes it necessary for him to report the denial of Peter before the trial, since that had to take place at night because of the cock crowing. (Compare Luke 22:67–71 preceded by vv. 56–65 with Mark 14:55–65 followed by vv. 66–72).

2. Luke makes no reference to a conviction, either of blasphemy or of any other kind, nor to a rending of garments, which agrees with the fact that nothing reported in connection wit the trial could have been grounds for convicting Jesus of blasphemy. In Luke the high priest merely says that no further witnesses are needed because Jesus himself said all that they needed to hear (v. 71). The significance of this statement is not totally clear, but what is clear is that compared with Mark, Luke carefully avoids mention of either conviction or blasphemy.

3. Luke also makes no reference to mistreatment of Jesus at the scene of the trial, because that is historically inconceivable. In Luke, Jesus is mistreated the night before the trial; those who took him into custody were responsible for the mistreatment. (Compare Luke 22:63–65

with Mark 14:65.) An interesting feature is that Luke reverses the guilt of blasphemy by attributing it to those who mocked Jesus (v. 65). Jesus was the object of the blasphemy, not the subject who blasphemed.

The following further differences between the three accounts are worth noting.

4. Luke omits the first part of the Markan account, that is, the preliminary hearing, Mark 14:55–61. His reason could have been because this first questioning produced nothing relevant for the conviction. Mark reports twice that the evidence of the witnesses was contradictory (vv. 56 and 59), which, as we know from point 10 above, disqualifies it.

5. Matthew was evidently also aware that contradictory evidence was invalid and therefore eliminated those references. But whereas in Mark these contradictions show up the falseness of the witnesses, disqualifying them from the point of view of the Sanhedrin, Matthew goes to the extreme of presenting the Sanhedrin itself as not only seeking witnesses that would testify against Jesus (which in itself already contradicts the sense of the directives for such a trial according to points 2, 5, and especially 13, above), but false witnesses at that (Matt. 26:59). This is a preposterous assumption, to say the least, especially if one considers the great concern about false testimony in capital cases in the Sanhedrin rules (see point 9 above). According to Matthew the Sanhedrin had difficulty finding such witnesses, but finally two did come forward and witness concerning the destruction and rebuilding of the temple (vv. 59–60). In Matthew this testimony leads to the next question concerning Jesus' messiahship (vv. 62–63). With typical editorial skill Matthew eliminated the loose ends of the Markan account and made it a tightly coherent description.

To sum up, in the first part of Mark we have a rather directionless preliminary questioning of Jesus (vv. 55–61), followed by the specific question to Jesus, "Are you the messiah, the Son of God?" (v. 61e) and Jesus' expanded affirmation of that charge (v. 62), which leads to his conviction for blasphemy (vv. 63–64). Matthew changed the preliminary questioning into a tightly coherent account (vv. 29–63a), which leads to the question concerning Jesus' messiahship and sonship of God (v. 63b–c). The rest of the account is not substantially different from Mark (cf. 64–66), but Matthew's view that the Sanhedrin itself sought false witnesses places his version of the trial in even greater contradiction of the rules set by the tractate *Sanhedrin*.

Luke disregarded Mark's preliminary questioning, probably because it contributed nothing to the progress of the trial. It should be remembered that he did not have Matthew's revised version in front of him. More significant is that the trial procedure in Luke's version is in much greater accord with the rules set by the tractate *Sanhedrin*; it occurs in the daytime, and the mistreatment is eliminated from the scene of the trial, as is any reference to a conviction for blasphemy. Also noteworthy is that Luke distinguishes the question concerning Jesus' messiahship (with the related reference to the Son of Man sitting at the right hand of God) from the question concerning Jesus' divine sonship. It is worth noting, furthermore, that Luke has eliminated the statement that they will see the Son of Man sitting at the right hand of God (cf. Mark 14:62c, //, "you will see"), changing it to a mere statement that the Son of Man will sit "now" at God's right hand (v. 69a). Luke probably made these changes because by his time it had become clear that none of those who had been present at the trial could have seen the Son of Man sitting at the right hand of God and coming with the clouds of heaven.

As we shall see later, evidence indicates strongly that Luke used an independent source or sources for many parts of his passion narrative. In the case of the trial before the Sanhedrin, however, indications are that he merely edited the Markan account, eliminating features that he determined to have been inaccurate and making it clear that the crucial issue had been Jesus' claim to be the Son of God. The "you say that I am" (v. 70) is merely another way of affirming that what had been asked was true, as the reaction of the high priest, "We ourselves have heard it from his mouth" (v. 71), clearly shows. As we will see below, other clues indicate that the Lukan version is indeed dependent on Mark.

An interesting feature of Luke's version of the story is how he expanded on Mark's simple "I am" (14:62) with Jesus' dual reply, "If I tell you, you will not believe [me]; and if I ask, you will not answer" (22:68–69) and "You say that I am" (v. 70). With his first reply Jesus calls the bluff of his questioners. Their question, "If you are the messiah, tell us?" (v. 67), is not genuine; they are not really looking for an answer. In his reply, without denying that he is the messiah, Jesus makes it clear that their question is a bluff. When they sarcastically conclude, "So you are then the Son of God?" (v. 70), Jesus, in effect, replies, "There you yourselves have said it, and whatever else I may answer is irrelevant to you." Even though Jesus replies to their questions, Luke makes it clear that Jesus has no illusions that it is a sincere discussion of what are among the most crucial issues in the entire series of events.

With all of this, however, we have clarified only the interrelationship between the three versions of the trial and the relationship of all three of them to the rules stipulated in the tractate *Sanhedrin*. The question of the nature of the blasphemy of which Jesus had been convicted remains. Luke identifies it as Jesus' claim to have been the Son of God, but he does not refer to it as blasphemy. He also does not say that Jesus was condemned to death, leaving that part altogether vague (cf. v. 71, also 23:2, the charge that the Jewish authorities brought to Pilate). In Luke it is the crowds who subsequently demand that Jesus be crucified, not the Jewish leaders

(23:21, cf. v. 18). Luke knew how it all ended, but obviously he did not want to commit himself to details about which he was uncertain.

Mark and Matthew both state that the conviction was for blasphemy, but what the blasphemy was remains historically unclear. Nothing Jesus said could have been taken as blasphemy in the sense of the tractate *Sanhedrin*. One could infer (it is not explicit) that Jesus referred to himself when he spoke of the Son of Man who was to sit at the right hand of God, but that too was not blasphemy. The claim to have been the messiah, the Son of God, could have been considered preposterous, but it was not blasphemous. *Son of God* was an appropriate title for the messiah who was to have been, like the kings of Israel and Judah, adopted by God as his son (cf. Ps. 2:7, "You are my son; this day I have generated you"). There were many messianic pretenders during the period immediately preceding and during the first centuries of the Christian era, and none of them was accused of blasphemy. The reference to the destruction and rebuilding of the temple leads nowhere in Mark because of the contradictory witnesses (v. 59), and although it leads up to the question of Jesus' messiahship in Matthew, as such it too is not blasphemy. In Mark and Matthew the statement is not a reference to the body of Jesus as in John 2:19–22. It should be noted, furthermore, that what Jesus said according to Mark 13:2, //s, "Not a stone will remain on a stone [of the temple] which will not be broken down," was an expectation shared by others, for example, believers in Jewish apocalypticism (*Ethiopic Enoch* 90:28, cf. Josephus, *Jewish Wars* 6.5.3), and even by the rabbis (Jerusalem Talmud, *Yoma* 43c).

The immediate reaction of the high priest to Jesus' statement concerning the Son of Man in Mark and Matthew gives the impression that Jesus' statement must have been the blasphemy, but it is unclear how that could have been the case. Luke ruled out that possibility completely by using the statement concerning the Son of Man only to lead up to the crucial question of Jesus being the Son of God.

D. THE BLASPHEMY OF JESUS (JOHN 10:30–39)

But if nothing Jesus said could have been grounds for convicting him of blasphemy in a Sanhedrin trial, from another perspective his claim to have been the Son of God could have been considered blasphemous by the Jews. In John 10:33 we read that when Jesus asked the Jews why they wanted to stone him, they replied that it was not for anything he had done, but "because you who are a human being put yourself forward as God." To this Jesus replied, "Is it not written in your Law, 'I say you are gods?' If [Scripture] calls those to whom the word of God was addressed gods, and the authority of Scripture cannot be dissolved, why do you say that he whom the Father sanctified and sent into the world blasphemes because I said 'I am the son of God?' " (vv. 34–36).

Indeed, as Jesus claims here in the Fourth Gospel, the designation *Son of God* could not have been considered blasphemous in Jewish circles since it was used widely in Scripture, for example, with regard to the messiah in Psalm 2:7 where God says to the psalmist, "You are my son, this day I have generated you." The expression also occurs in Psalm 89:27 with reference to David, "He will say to me, 'You are my father, my God, and the rock of my salvation.' Indeed, I will make him [my] firstborn, and raise him above all kings of the earth." It is also used for Israel in Exodus 4:22–23, "You should say to Pharaoh, 'The Lord says, Israel is my firstborn son, therefore I demand: Let my son go!' " and for the heavenly beings of Genesis 6:2–3.

On the other hand, Jews in the time of Jesus had become concerned that the expression might be taken in a literal sense. Thus the pronouncement in Psalm 2:7, "You are my son; this day I have generated you," is translated interpretively into Aramaic in the Targum, "You are dear to me as a son to his father; innocent as if I have created you this day." By interpreting metaphorically the expression in the psalm, the Targum translation made clear that the person addressed in the psalm (the messiah) was not literally the son of God. It is precisely such a literal understanding of Jesus as Son of God that we find in the story of his divine generation in Matthew 1:18–25 and Luke 1:26–38. The conception of a divine generation through a young woman was widespread in **Hellenistic** antiquity.

The Targum translation of Psalm 2:7 also guarded against the similarly unacceptable conception of the sonship of God in the sense of preexistence, such as we find in Philippians 2:6–7, "He who existed as a God [literally, "in the form of God"] did not consider it as plunder to be equal to God, but emptied himself [of his divinity] and became a human being [literally, "took on the form of a slave"]."

The designation *Son of God*, which could have been used without problems in inner Jewish circles, took on new connotations when Gentile Christians applied it to Jesus in the literal sense of a divine generation or of his preexistence. John 10:33 reveals that the designation in this literal sense was indeed considered blasphemous by the Jews, even if not in the technical, legal sense defined by the tractate *Sanhedrin* 7:5.

Thus, improbable as the Gospel accounts of Jesus' trial before the Sanhedrin appear historically, they become understandable when we consider them in the context of the subsequent encounter between Gentile Christianity and its Jewish opponents. The accounts of Jesus' trial before the Sanhedrin should not be approached with the question of historically accurate reporting of the actual incident in mind; they represent the perspective of the first decades of Gentile Christianity in which the story of the trial was interpreted in terms of what had become the most crucial issue between Jews and Christians, the understanding that Jesus was the son of God in the sense of either his divine generation or his preexistence. The Gospel accounts reveal that early Christianity understood this issue to have been fundamental already in the conflict between Jesus and the Jewish authorities in Jerusalem. In the setting of the conflict between Jews and Christians in the first decades of Gentile Christianity, Luke's reversal of the accusation of blasphemy gains in effectiveness: "And blaspheming, they said many other things to him" (Luke 22:65). It was not blasphemy to call Jesus the Son of God, but to mock him who was truly the Son of God was indeed blasphemy.

If, according to the Gospel tradition, Jesus' claim to have been the Son of God was the blasphemy of which he was found guilty, the question remains why, according to Mark and Matthew, the high priest waited to rend his garments and to pronounce the guilty verdict until after Jesus made the statement concerning the Son of Man. If the blasphemy was Jesus' affirmation that he was the Son of God, the reference to the Son of Man can be understood only as an interpretive extension that interrupts the flow of the story. It clarifies in what sense Jesus' claim to have been the messiah, the Son of God, had to be understood, that is, not as a political figure who had been destined to liberate Israel from Roman rule, but as the Son of Man who was to come on the clouds of heaven as God's eschatological representative.

This interpretative extension was added later. In the original version of the story the reaction of the high priest must have followed directly on Jesus' affirmation that he was the Son of God, a sequence that Luke reestablished in his version of the story (cf. vv. 70–71). The presence of the reference to the Son of Man in Luke reveals that he, like Matthew, must have used Mark's version in this part of his passion narrative, since it was probably Mark himself who interpreted Jesus' affirmation that he was the Son of God by means of the insertion concerning the Son of Man. As we have seen, he interpreted Peter's confession of Jesus as messiah in a similar way by means of the first prediction of the passion in 8:27–33.

The reference to the Son of Man is drawn from three Old Testament passages. "You will see" is quoted from Zechariah 12:10, "And they will see him whom they pierced." In Revelation 1:7 we have an explicit connection between Jesus coming as the Son of Man on the clouds of heaven and all eyes will see him, those who pierced him." (Cf. also Matt. 24:30 and John 19:37.) As is well known, "sitting at the right hand" comes from Psalm 110:1, and "the Son of Man coming on the clouds of heaven" from Daniel 7:13. This expansion of Jesus' affirmation that he was the messiah, the Son of God, was not arbitrary. It was formulated by quoting Scripture passages that clarified the meaning of Jesus and that of his messiahship. Luke, evidently not recognizing that "you will see" was a reference to Zechariah 12:10, eliminated the statement because he was aware that none of those present at the trial would actually have seen Jesus sitting at the right hand of God and coming on the clouds of heaven.

The basis of Mark's account of Jesus' trial before the Sanhedrin thus appears to have been a Gentile Christian tradition based on the conviction that the decisive issue between Christians and Jews in the first decades of Christianity, the claim that Jesus had been the Son of God, had also been the reason for his conviction for blasphemy and his condemnation to death. Mark himself apparently added to this tradition the expansion of Jesus' reply to the high priest's question by quoting from Scripture passages that clarified the meaning of Jesus' messiahship.

In this case Matthew followed Mark rather closely, but Luke made a number of changes. He divided the exchange between the high priest and Jesus into two parts to bring out more clearly that the decisive issue had been Jesus' sonship of God. Luke also made other changes, evidently based on knowledge of the rules that the Sanhedrin would have been required to follow in a capital case such as blasphemy. Luke appears to have been aware that blasphemy in a legal sense had not been committed, that a guilty verdict in a capital case could not have been rendered on the same day, and that, in fact, what was reported could not have been a Sanhedrin trial of a capital case at all.

It is important, finally, to note yet another violation of the rules for a trial in which the accused had been convicted of blasphemy. Such a person had to be stoned (*Sanh.* 7:5) and then hung with hands tied together over a wooden beam (*Sanh.* 6:4). It is inconceivable that the Sanhedrin, having convicted Jesus of blasphemy, would have handed him over to the Romans for execution on some other charge, nor would the Romans have executed anyone for blasphemy of the Jewish God at the bidding of the Sanhedrin. The fact that Jesus was executed by the Romans because he claimed to have been the king of the Jews (Mark 15:26, //s) suggests that something else was at stake.

Conclusion. We have succeeded in getting a clearer picture of the possible history of the tradition of Jesus' trial before the Sanhedrin, and of the way that tradition was handled in the Gospels. With regard to what may actually have happened, however, we have come up with only a negative conclusion: whatever transpired between Jesus and the Sanhedrin could not have been a trial in which Jesus was convicted of blasphemy. Luke, although retaining most of the material from this part of Mark, already came to a similar conclusion. According to his version of the events, Jesus was not formally convicted of anything; blasphemy is not even mentioned.

What happened between Jesus and the Sanhedrin remains an unanswered question. Before we can address that question we need to gather further information from our Gospel sources.

CHAPTER 5

The Execution of Jesus as a Messianic Pretender

In the previous chapter we concluded that if Jesus had been convicted of blasphemy he should have been stoned to death (*Sanh.* 7:5) and hung with his hands tied together over a wooden beam (*Sanh.* 6:4). Because this did not happen, and Jesus was crucified instead by the Romans (cf. Mark 15:26, //s), we may conclude that he had probably not been found guilty of blasphemy in a trial before the Sanhedrin as described in the Gospels. Something else must have been going on.

According to the Gospels, the Romans crucified Jesus as a messianic pretender, that is, as someone who had claimed to have been the king of the Jews with the objective of leading an insurrection to liberate the Jews from Roman rule.

In this section we will investigate what light the Gospel accounts of the events leading up to Jesus' execution as a messianic pretender might shed on these last phases of his life. A basic question is what reason the Romans could have had to convict and execute. In order to find an answer to this question we will consider the following material: (A) the plot against Jesus (Mark 11:18, //; 14:1–2, 10–11, 18–21, 43–52, //s; Luke 22:35–38; cf. Matt. 27:3–10); (B) the actions of the Romans (Mark 15:1–26, //s); (C) the entry into Jerusalem and the cleansing of the temple (Mark 11:1–10, 15–19, //s); and (D) the predicament of the Jewish authorities (John 11:47–53).

A. THE PLOT AGAINST JESUS (MARK 14:1–52, //s)

The texts to which we will give our primary attention here (Mark 11:18; 12:12; 14:1–2, 10–11, 18–21, 43–52, //s; and Luke 22:35–38) all concern the plot against Jesus and the part played by his betrayer. There is reason to believe that of these, Mark 14:1–2 (#305), 10–11 (#307), and 43–52 (#331) originally formed a single tradition. This tradition will be our most important source in trying to uncover what transpired between the Jewish leaders and Jesus. Mark 11:18 (#274) is duplicated by 14:1–2 and may have been formulated by Mark himself as a way of identifying the cleansing of the temple (11:15–17, //s, #273) as the immediate reason for the plot against Jesus. Whatever the reasons for its origin, Mark 11:18 does not add anything not found in 14:1–2, and we do not need to consider it further here. Mark 12:12 (#278) establishes continuity between 11:18 and 14:1–2 and thus between the tradition of the cleansing of the temple (11:15–17) and of the plot against Jesus (14:1–2, 10–11, 43–52). (The first mention of a plot against Jesus actually occurs in 3:6, but that was a different plot, by the Pharisees and the Herodians. They were not involved in the final events of Jesus' life in Mark, for which specifically the chief priests and the elders were responsible.)

That 14:1–2 and 10–11 may originally have belonged together is made almost certain by the fact that what now separates them, the anointing of Jesus in Bethany (vv. 3–9), is an independent tradition that can be found in a different version and setting in the Gospel of Luke (7:36–50, #114). It is also reported by John in yet another version (John 12:1–8, #267). Without this interruption Mark 14:1–2 and 10–11 form a tight material unity. The Jewish leaders seek a way to take Jesus captive that would avoid turmoil among the people at the feast (vv. 1–2); they accept when Judas offers to assist them in this endeavor (vv. 10–11). Judas then seeks an appropriate moment to lead those charged with the arrest to Jesus. We know from vv. 43–52 that the moment arrives when Jesus is in Gethsemane, away from the crowds.

As the Markan account now stands, Judas's two actions—his search for the appropriate moment to betray Jesus (vv. 10–11) and that moment's arrival (vv. 43–45)—are separated from one another by the intervening accounts of the events leading up to and including the institution of the Lord's Supper (vv. 12–25) and of Jesus in Gethsemane (vv. 26–42). These intervening verses also contain Jesus' identification of Judas as the betrayer (vv. 18–21, #310), but this does not appear to have belonged to the tradition of the conspiracy and Judas's part in it (that is, vv. 1–2, 10–11, 43–52). The identification of the betrayer appears to be an independent tradition that Luke uses in a different version after the institution of the Lord's Supper (22:21–23, #312), as opposed to Mark (followed by Matthew), who places it before the institution. John also reports the incident in yet another version (John 13:21–30, #310). The focus in all versions of this tradition is on the identity of the betrayer, whereas in Mark 14:1–2, 10–11, and 43–52 it is on the plot against Jesus and Judas's part in it.

One does not *have to* take verses 1–2, 10–11, and 43–52 as an original unity. However one takes these verses, they show that the Jews sought to take Jesus into custody quietly (vv. 1–2), that Judas offered his services to them (vv. 10–11), and that with his help they succeeded in their objective (vv. 43–52). Nevertheless, as far as the interpretation of the history of the Gospel traditions is concerned, nothing favors the assumption that Mark consistently incorporated whole traditions unchanged into his Gospel. He may on occasion have separated traditions that belonged to the same temporal sequence and interwove them with other traditions, thus providing a multilayered account, as appears to have been the case here.

Later we will be concerned with the Judas traditions. Our main concern at the moment is those texts that shed light on the actions and motives of the Jewish leaders, that is, the series, Mark 14:1–2, 10–11, and 43–52, //s. First we have to investigate the way in which this material was handled by the evangelists. In Luke the report of the Jewish leaders' intention to arrest Jesus (Luke 22:1–2) is followed immediately by Judas's offer of assistance (vv. 3–6), which presumably was the original sequence in the tradition. However, in itself, this order in Luke does not necessarily lend support to the presumption of an original unity. He may have left out the anointing of Jesus in Bethany at this point because he had already quoted a different version of the same tradition earlier in his Gospel (7:36–50).

Luke deviates from Mark in a number of ways in recounting the events that took place between Judas's offer of assistance and the arrest of Jesus (22:7–46). First, as we noted above, he names a different location for the identification of the betrayer. Furthermore, Luke places the prediction of Peter's denial before Jesus and his disciples leave for Gethsemane, whereas Mark has it on the way there (compare Luke 22:31–34, 39 with Mark 14:26–31). Luke also leaves out some of the Markan material, for example, some of what Jesus said on the way to the Mount of Olives (Mark 14:26–27, //), and adds some of his own—the discussion of precedence among the disciples and the reward of discipleship (22:24–3, #313) and the discussion concerning the two swords (22:35–38, #316). The first of these two additions is paralleled in different versions and in different locations in each of the other three Gospels (cf. Mark 10:41–45; Matt. 20:24–28; 19:28; John 13:4–5, 12–17). This evidence confirms: (1) that the passion narrative was not a solid unity but a collection of individual traditions, the sequence of which had not been fixed; and (2) that Luke did not depend heavily on Mark in this part of his Gospel.

With regard specifically to the three sections under discussion, Luke and Mark have little verbal agreement, whereas Matthew follows Mark closely, as we shall note below. The only verbal agreements of significance between Luke and Mark are the following: (1) Luke agrees with Mark against Matthew that it is the Jewish leaders, not Judas, who brought up the question of payment for Judas's services (cf. Mark 14:11, //s); (2) Luke agrees substantially with Mark in the verbal formulation of the statement about Jesus' captors going out with swords and sticks and Jesus' daily appearances in the temple (Mark 14:48–49, //s), as does Matthew. However, these agreements are such that one cannot definitely conclude from them that Luke quoted from Mark. The wording of the statement about Judas's request for money is the most natural way to express the idea, and Jesus' statement about his captors may already have become relatively fixed in its oral form. On the other hand, we can assume that Luke did have Mark available as a source when he wrote his Gospel, so that he could conceivably have made use of it at certain points in this part of his Gospel but gone his own way at others.

In view of the fact that Luke includes so much material of his own in this part of the passion narrative, even in places where he could have quoted from Mark, and that there is so little verbal agreement between him and Mark in the three sections that concern us here, it appears highly probable that he had access to additional source materials for these three sections. If he did, that would tend to support the conception of an original unity of the tradition of Mark 14:1–2 and 10–11, //s, since Luke presents it as a unity. And if 14:1–2 and 10–11 formed one tradition, we would have to conclude that it included verses 43–52 as well, since these verses form the necessary conclusion to the earlier verses.

Matthew adhered closely to Mark in this entire portion of his Gospel. The fact that Matthew presents the same material in the same sequence as Mark is evidence of his heavy dependence on Mark. His only significant changes occur in precisely those parts that concern us here. His parallel to Mark 14:1–2 is expanded with a Son of Man saying (26:2b) and information concerning the place where the leaders met to discuss the plot (v. 3). In the parallel to Mark 14:10–11 he writes that Judas requested a fee for his services (26:15), whereas Mark, with whom Luke agrees in this case, writes that the leaders offered the money.

Matthew also reports the amount involved, thirty silver pieces (26:15), probably based on the understanding that the betrayal was in fulfillment of Zechariah 11:12–13, which he quotes in the same connection in 27:9 (#335). Matthew probably also drew the information that Judas requested the money from the Zechariah passage that reads in the relevant portion, "And I said, 'If it please you, then give me my wages; if not, then let it be.' And they weighed out as my wages thirty silver pieces" (v. 12). Zechariah 11:12 explicitly states that the betrayer requested the payment. (Scripture influenced traditions about Jesus to such an extent that if it had become clear that a passage was fulfilled in a specific incident in Jesus' life, early Christianity took it for granted that additional information about that incident could be drawn from the same passage. We will see this especially in the case of Jesus' entry into Jerusalem. It was assumed that the prophet saw more than even an observer of the incident could have seen.)

Finally, Matthew changed Mark 14:43–52 by adding the saying about those who take up the sword perishing by the sword and that God could have sent legions to Jesus' aid if he had requested it (26:52–54). Like Luke, he left out the reference to the incident of the young man who fled naked (Mark 14:51–52).

Notwithstanding these changes, Matthew appears to have depended on

Mark for all of these sections, including 26:1–5, where, however, he probably also drew partly from another source. If we exclude Matthew's insertion of verses 52–54, there is an exceptionally high degree of verbal agreement between Matthew 26:47–56 and Mark.

A number of features in connection with the scene of Jesus' actual apprehension have not yet been discussed. To these we now turn.

Judas's betrayal of Jesus with a kiss, reported by all three synoptic evangelists, is a legendary dramatization of his reprehensible act. The kiss is almost certainly not historical and receives no mention in John (cf. John 18:3–5). A slight but nevertheless bloody skirmish must have taken place that ended with the flight of the disciples. One cannot assume that everyone looked on kindly as one of the disciples (identified by John as Peter) cut off the ear of the high priest's slave (identified by John as Malchus), an incident reported by all four evangelists. Luke could in this case have depended on Mark, but John's use of an independent source reveals it to have been a well-known story.

All the evangelists except Mark explicitly dissociate Jesus from the violent action. According to Luke, Jesus put a stop to further hostility with the command, "Let it be; up to here!" (v. 51), evidently meaning "this is enough," whereupon he healed the damage to the slave's ear. On the other hand, Luke has Jesus tacitly approve the presence of swords in Gethsemane (22:35–38, #316). The discussion concerning the two swords contains two opposed parts. In verses 36–37 Jesus encourages the disciples to arm themselves, whereas verse 38 sets a limit on the acquisition of swords; two are sufficient. Luke apparently used a tradition according to which Jesus had reversed himself, "And he said to them, 'When I sent you out without a purse or bag or sandals, did you lack anything?' And they said, 'Nothing.' And he said to them, 'Now, whoever has a purse, take it, and likewise a bag, and whoever does not, sell his mantle, and purchase a sword' " (22:36–37). All the Gospels know that the disciples were armed in Gethsemane, but here Jesus himself encourages them to do so. It is not a favorable picture of Jesus, so Luke evidently tried to counterbalance its effect with the statement that the two swords were enough to emphasize the limits set by Jesus, similar to his statement in Gethsemane to end hostilities, "Let it be; up to here!" (v. 51). The discussion of swords, however, does suggest that a confrontation was expected when Jesus and the disciples made their way to the garden. Such an expectation is made certain by the disciples' actual possession of swords in Gethsemane. Even though all of this does not prove that Jesus was actually a messianic pretender, it remains unfavorable to the traditional view that he was not involved as a messiah in a movement of armed resistance against Rome.

In both Matthew and John Jesus commands the person who wielded the sword with which the ear of the high priest's slave had been cut off to put it back into its sheath. Furthermore, both indicate in different ways that Jesus accepted the necessity of what was taking place (Matt. 26:52–

54; John 18:11). According to John, Jesus requested the safe retreat of his followers even before the bloodletting (18:8).

In all four Gospels Jesus is presented with supreme dignity, above all involvement at the earthly level of the events. This tendency in the Gospels, less pronounced in Mark than in the others, obscures what his real attitude toward these events may have been. What does come through in all the accounts is that the disciples were not unprepared for the confrontation, but that they were no match for the odds against them. The mood of calm that now pervades the scene, created by the controlled dignity of Jesus as reported by all four evangelists, is deceptive. A bloody confrontation that ended with the flight of the disciples was what evidently took place. With regard to Jesus, we have to assume that he had given at least tacit approval to the preparations that led to the skirmish, as Luke reports in the discussion concerning the two swords (22:35–38). However, we have no reason at this point to believe that these preparations involved a planned uprising against Rome.

The second most important character in these events was Judas. Who was this man? More precisely, what was his relationship to Jesus?

Judas is firmly established in the tradition as one of the twelve (cf. Mark 3:19, //s; 14:10 //s; John 6:71; 12:4, etc., also Acts 1:16, 25), yet there is good reason to doubt the historical correctness of this tradition. 1 Corinthians 15:3b–5, the oldest written tradition of the resurrection, states that the resurrected Christ appeared first to Peter, "then to the twelve" (v. 5). According to this very old tradition Judas could not have been one of the twelve. The fact that "twelve" in 1 Corinthians 15:5 was changed to "eleven" in some early manuscripts reveals that the contradiction was recognized very early.

That Matthew 19:28 and 16:18–19 are presented as precrucifixion events has no historical significance. The traditions were originally handed down as single units or small collections without any indication whether a tradition concerned something that took place during Jesus' life on earth or was something that occurred after his resurrection, except what could be inferred from a particular tradition itself. The evangelists had to try to determine this for themselves, and the fact that they were largely concerned with the life of Jesus on earth resulted in their placing many traditions that originally concerned the resurrected Christ in their accounts of his life on earth. We will encounter more such cases, the most significant probably being the transfiguration on the mountain (Mark 9:2–10, //s, #161). We have no reason to assume that every incident reported by the Gospels as having taken place during the earthly life of Jesus was also understood in that way in the tradition, unless internal evidence in the particular story itself demands that it be taken as such. The placement of the traditions in the Gospels is of no historical consequence.

The above considerations concerning "the twelve," corroborated by the specific evidence of 1 Corinthians 15:5, make it improbable that Judas could have been one of the twelve. He probably gained this position and his seat at the Last Supper as a result of the understanding that through him Psalm 41:10 was fulfilled: "He who eats my bread raised his heel against me" (cf. John 13:18, #309). The understanding of him as one of the original twelve subsequently called for the tradition that he had been replaced by Matthias in the postresurrection body of the twelve, as told by Luke in Acts 1:15–26. There, as in 1 Corinthians 15:5, the understanding is that the twelve represented persons to whom the resurrected Christ had appeared, as verse 22 explicitly states. The development of the tradition concerning Judas also explains a slight incongruity in the synoptic passion narratives, from which one gets the impression that Judas was still with the others when they arrived at Gethsemane (cf. Mark 14:26, //s, which gives no indication that Judas had left the group) until he suddenly appears as if from nowhere with those who came to arrest Jesus (Mark 14:43, //s). The Fourth Gospel avoids this incongruity; after the identification of the betrayer the evangelist informs the reader, "Taking the morsel that man left immediately. And it was night" (13:30).

This does not necessarily mean that Judas may not have been an intimate of Jesus. He must have had sufficient knowledge of Jesus' coming and going to arrange for him to be taken into custody inconspicuously. That it had been necessary for him to identify Jesus in the small group that had gathered in Gethsemane reveals that Jesus was not known to everyone, as the Gospel accounts may lead one to believe. The correct identification of Jesus was crucial for the authorities. If the wrong person had been apprehended their plan could have backfired. Judas was critically important for them.

Tradition holds that Judas met an ignoble death, but the stories do not agree on the way he died. According to Matthew 27:3–10 (#355) he committed suicide by hanging himself, but according to Acts 1:18 he fell headlong and burst open, his intestines flowing out. Both traditions link his death with a piece of land in Jerusalem that was called "field of blood," but they do not agree on the way he became linked to it. This suggests that the traditions were based on a legend explaining the origin of the name of the plot of land (an **etiological legend**). It is a legend which had not been firmly established with regard to the details. Acts reports that Judas himself bought the land with the money he received for the betrayal. Matthew treats him slightly more sympathetically, reporting that he tried to undo his evil work even before Jesus was crucified (vv. 3–4), and when he did not succeed he tried to disassociate himself from it by throwing the money into the temple. In the end he hung himself in despair (v. 5), and the Jewish leaders used his money to buy the plot of land. As we have seen, Matthew's version was heavily influenced by his reading of Zechariah 11:12–13.

From all of the above we may conclude that the Jewish authorities had planned and successfully carried out the arrest of Jesus with the aid of someone from the circle of Jesus' acquaintances. Furthermore, we may conclude that the followers of Jesus were not a completely defenseless, docile group, but they were probably outnumbered, certainly outwitted by the deceit of the man we ahve come to know as Judas. We still do not know why the Jewish authorities wanted to have Jesus arrested or what Jesus' own position in all of this was although the tradition that his followers had been prepared for an armed confrontation in Gethsemane indicates that he may have been involved in a messianic movement.

In order to answer these questions we turn next to the Roman authorities and specifically to the procurator, Pilate, who was responsible for the decision to have Jesus executed. What may the reasons have been for his decision?

B. THE ACTIONS OF THE ROMANS (MARK 15:1–26, //s)

A striking incongruity in the trial before Pilate (Mark 15:1–5, //s, #334 and #336) is that after Jesus had already accepted the charge on which he was subsequently executed (v. 2, cf. 26, //s), Pilate still expressed amazement that Jesus did not reply to the charges that were brought against him (v. 4). Why would Pilate have been concerned about the vague allegations (v. 3) and Jesus's unwillingness to reply to them (vv. 4–5) when Jesus had already accepted the charge that brought him the death penalty?

Also noteworthy are the formal parallels between this trial and the one before the Sanhedrin. Some events appear in reverse order, however, as the following table shows. The translations are literal, to bring out parallel wording, which appears in boldface print. Italics indicate the same meanings expressed in different formulations.

Mark 14:60–62a	*Mark 15:2, 4–5*
v. 60 And standing up in their midst the high priest asked Jesus; **You reply nothing**? *How these do witness against you!*	v. 4 And Pilate again asked him, saying, **You reply nothing**? *Look with what they accuse you.*
v. 61 **But** he remained silent and *did not reply* **anything**.	v. 5 **But** Jesus *no longer replied* **anything**, so that Pilate was amazed.
Again the high priest **asked him** and said to him, **Are you** *the messiah*, the Son of God?	v. 2 And Pilate **asked him**, **Are you** *the king of the Jews?*
v. 26 And Jesus said, *I am.*	And answering him he said, *You say it.*

The sequence in the Sanhedrin trial and Jesus' silence until the crucial question is asked makes good sense, unlike the trial before Pilate. It is nevertheless improbably that the version of the trial before Pilate was merely copied from the Sanhedrin trial with some reshuffling of the material. The similarities and somewhat incongruous order in the story of the trial before Pilate can be explained better as the result of early Christians working with a double motif in their understanding of what happened at both trials, namely, that Jesus remained silent with regard to all charges except for his affirmation of the charge that he was the messiah. In the Markan version of the trial before Pilate the two parts of the motif are presented in an inverse order. This also tells us something about the way early Christians worked with their materials. They were obviously more concerned with the exposition of the dual motif than with a meaningful development in the sequence of the events. In their minds the same double motif applied to both trials. All charges against Jesus were irrelevant, except the one on which he was convicted, namely, that he was the messiah.

The acceptance of the single charge of being the messiah had three very different but important effects from the point of view of early Christianity. It clarified

1. why Jesus had been condemned to death by the Sanhedrin—because from the point of view of the Sanhedrin he had committed blasphemy (Mark 14:61–64, //s).
2. why the Romans convicted and executed him as king of the Jews—because they took him for a messianic pretender with the intention of leading an uprising against Rome (Mark 15:26, cf. v. 15, //s).

Furthermore, it reaffirmed

3. that Jesus was indeed the messiah, the Son of God in the early Christian sense of the term, for example, in the sense of the Son of Man (Mark 14:62, //s). See in this regard Jesus' disclaimer in John 18:36, "My kingdom is not of this earth."

The one term *messiah* meant something different in each case, but it was sufficient in itself to clarify all three attitudes toward Jesus.

In the actual account of the trial before Pilate (Mark 15:1–5, 15, //s), Matthew once again followed Mark closely, except for editorial changes (for example, 27:12 compared with Mark 15:3) and two additions: reference to the dream of Pilate's wife (v. 19), and the scene in which Pilate washes his hands in innocence of the blood of Jesus and in which the people claim responsibility for themselves and in the name of their children (vv. 24–25). The addition of this scene by Matthew is part of a process in Christianity in which the blame for the execution of Jesus was placed increasingly on the Jewish people, while every attempt at least at this stage, was made to exonerate the Roman authorities. According to Matthew, Pilate realized that everything was futile and that if he did not accede to the wishes of the Jews matters would only get worse (v. 24). As we will see, this process is represented in a different way in Luke and even in Mark, although in his case still hesitantly (cf. Mark 15:10, 14).

Luke once more went his own way, except in the formulation of Pilate's crucial question whether Jesus was the king of the Jews, and in Jesus's reply, which is verbally quite similar to Mark (cf. Mark 15:2, //s). In Luke's narrative the chief priests do not come with vague allegations as in Mark, "And the chief priests accused him of many things" (Mark 15:3). They bring specific charges: "We found this man misguiding our people, hindering tribute to be paid to Caesar, and saying that he is the royal messiah" (23:2), and they stick to this accusation against every protest of Pilate (cf. v. 5). It is surprising that after Jesus admitted to the crucial charge of being the king of the Jews (cf. v. 3), Luke has Pilate argue Jesus' innocence, declaring, "I find no fault in this man" (v. 4). In the end, however, Pilate bowed to their demands and "gave Jesus over to the Jews' wishes" (v. 25). Notwithstanding this weakness in Pilate, it is important from the standpoint of the early Christian tradition that as a Roman judge he pronounced Jesus innocent of the charge against him.

The tradition of the trial and execution of Jesus by the Romans attracted to itself a number of other traditions, which appear already in Mark: (1) The release of Barabbas (Mark 15:14–16, //s) presented as having been in conformity with a custom of setting a prisoner free at the feast (cf. Mark 15:6, //s, also John 18:39), but there is no evidence for such a practice in either Jewish or Roman sources. One can only wonder at the irony of Barabbas having been in prison for complicity in a violent uprising (cf. Mark 15:7, Luke 23:19) and then set free, and Jesus innocently convicted and executed on a similar charge. According to John, Barabbas was a robber (John 18:40). (2) The mocking of Jesus by the soldiers (Mark 15:16–20a, //). This incident is absent from Luke, possibly intentionally. In Luke, Pilate tells the Jews that he is willing to have Jesus beaten but that he would then let him go free (23:16). (3) The legend of Simon of Cyrene being forced to help carry the cross of Jesus (Mark 15:20b–21, //s). (4) The tradition concerning the dividing of Jesus' clothes, which is quoted literally from Psalm 22:19 (Mark 15:24, //s).

Matthew wove two apparently related legends into his account, as already mentioned above: (1) The dream of Pilate's wife (27:19), and (2) Pilate washing his hands to demonstrate his innocence and the people taking responsibility for the blood of Jesus (vv. 24–25).

Luke added the following: (1) The story of Pilate sending Jesus to Herod (23:6–12). This may be a tradition developed from Psalm 2:2 according to which "the kings of the earth stood side by side and the rulers gathered together against the Lord and against his anointed one" (cf. Acts 4:26–27). (2) The incident with the women mourning Jesus on the way to Golgotha (23:27–31), which in its present form is a *vaticinium ex eventu*, a prophecy after the event, that is, of the destruction of Jerusalem in A.D. 70, effectively placed here in the mouth of Jesus.

From our discussion of the accounts of Jesus' trial before Pilate and his execution, it has become clear that a tendency developed to shift the blame for the crucifixion exclusively onto the Jews and to have Pilate testify to his innocence, even though Jesus had actually accepted the charge on which he was subsequently executed (cf. Mark 15:26, //s). We have little if any reason to doubt that historically Pilate did find Jesus guilty of the offense. The question is, on what grounds did he come to such a verdict? Indications are that the Jewish authorities (the chief priests and elders) were involved in bringing the charge against Jesus, but only Luke and John explicitly name it—that Jesus was a messianic pretender (Luke 23:2, 5; John 19:12). On the basis of this charge he was found guilty and executed. What grounds could there have been to suspect Jesus of this pretension? And why would the Jewish authorities have handed him over to the Romans on such a charge? The story of Jesus' entry into Jerusalem and the cleansing of the temple may provide an answer to the first question, and John 11:47–53 may help us answer the second.

C. THE ENTRY INTO JERUSALEM AND THE CLEANSING OF THE TEMPLE (MARK 11:1–10, 15–17, //s; #269 and #273)

If Jesus entered Jerusalem as described in the Gospels, such an incident could have made the Jewish leaders apprehensive about him as a messianic pretender. The Gospel event has every appearance of the public display of a messianic movement. The description so resembles the triumphant entry of a messianic pretender that the German scholar Hugo Gressmann proposed that it must have been the story of the Galilean political messiah Menahem ben Hiskia reported by Josephus in his *Jewish Wars* (2. 17.8–9), a story then applied to Jesus. (Josephus has "ben Judah," who had been the son of Hiskia. The designation "ben Hiskia" thus refers to his grandfather). This led Rudolf Bultmann to retort that if a messianic entry was possible in the case of Menahem, why should it not have been possible in the case of Jesus? (*History of the Synoptic Tradition*, p. 262 n. 2).

The present account appears to be a legend drawn in part from prophecy in Scripture. The question is, what basis did it have in history? The narrative has two parts: (1) the story of the miraculous acquisition of the donkey (Mark 11:1–6, //s), and (2) the actual story of the entry (vv. 7–10, //s). The latter is probably the older part, its extraordinary character having called forth the development of the former, which heightened the extraordinary nature of the entire incident even more.

The description of the acquisition of the donkey has some of the characteristic features of a Gospel miracle story: First, the preparation, in which it becomes clear that the achievement of the intended purpose could only be miraculous (vv. 1–3). Second, the actual performance of the miracle, in this case described in terms of the actions of the disciples (vv. 4–6). In a sense it is a dual miracle which describes, not only the extraordinary way in which the needed donkey became available (vv. 5–6), but also Jesus' exceptional knowledge of all that was to have happened. As Luke states, "They found it as Jesus described it to them" (19:32).

A third characteristic typical of Gospel miracle stories, the expression of awed recognition by the spectators, is absent from this part of the story. Note the dispassionate "and they allowed them" (v. 6b) with which this part of the story concludes in Mark. Possibly the rejoicing recognition of the crowds at Jesus' entry into Jerusalem takes the place of the characteristic awed recognition in a miracle story. In that way the unity of the narrative is established. The miracle story is not complete until the crowds rejoice at the entry of Jesus into Jerusalem.

The most difficult historical problem of the story is that its formulation is based almost entirely on Zechariah 9:9, which mentions not only the donkey, but also the entry of a king and the rejoicing crowds. Furthermore, the actual words of the crowds, "Blessed is he who comes in the name of the Lord" (v. 10, //s), were well known to every Jew: Psalm 118, from which they come, was part of the Hallel, the chanting of Psalms 113–118 at various Jewish feasts. As such, these words could have been the joyous greeting for every pilgrim who entered the gates of the city. In the tradition of Mark 11:7–10, //s, however, they are understood to apply specifically to Jesus, and they refer not merely to his coming to the feast, but to his coming "in the name of the Lord" in the special sense of the messiah. This is underscored in the words following immediately in Mark, "Blessed is the coming kingdom of our father David" (v. 10b), which were left out by Matthew and Luke but confirmed by John with his "and [blessed is] the kingdom of Israel" (12:13).

Matthew and Luke both follow Mark closely in this narrative. One potentially significant change is that both omit the reference to the blessed coming of the kingdom "of our father David" (Mark 11:10b). Did they leave it out independently of each other because they both considered the reference to David's kingdom inappropriate since it had a political connotation? On the other hand, the fact that it is absent from both could mean that it was added in an edition of Mark later than what Matthew and Luke used. We cannot be sure either way.

Matthew actually quoted Zechariah 9:9, introduced with the formula we encountered earlier in the stories of Jesus' birth and infancy, "This happened in order that the saying [of the Lord] through the prophet should be fulfilled, which says . . ." (v. 4). Matthew would not have encountered difficulty in finding the relevant passage here since, as we already noted, the description itself in Mark was drawn largely from Zechariah 9:9.

An interesting feature of Matthew's version is that he has Jesus sit on both donkeys, "And he sat upon them" (v. 7c). The Revised Standard Version neatly overcomes this difficulty by formulating, "And he sat thereon," thereby producing a more meaningful text but a false translation. Matthew probably did not try to envisage how Jesus "sat upon them." For him it was sufficient that Scripture said that the messiah was mounted "on a donkey and on the foal of an animal of burden" (cf. v. 5).

A further incident that could also have had messianic significance is the cleansing of the temple (Mark 11:15–17, //s). According to Mark it occurred on the day after the entry, but in Matthew and Luke it took place on the same day. Mark does have Jesus go up to the temple on the same day, but he only "[takes note] of everything" (11:11). John, as is well known, places the cleansing of the temple at the beginning of the ministry of Jesus (2:13–17, #25). The two incidents—royal entry and temple cleansing—could originally have been linked, similar to their linking in the story of Menahem ben Judah who, after entering Jerusalem as a king and successfully besieging the palace, also went up to the temple with pomp, to worship in royal attire attended by his followers in arms. In his case, however, that marked the beginning of his downfall (Josephus, *Jewish Wars*, 2.17.8–9). On the other hand, the fact that John places the cleansing in the beginning of his Gospel suggests that the two events may have been unrelated in the tradition.

The appearance of the same story in a completely different version in John indicates that it was a well-established tradition. (The same is true of the story of the entry.) The two versions agree in reporting that it was an action against the traders and the moneychangers in the temple complex. If the story is based on an actual incident it remains impossible to infer with any degree of certainty what may actually have happened. Mark, followed by Matthew, and in agreement with John, presents it as a large-scale incident in which Jesus acted alone. Luke tones down the scale of the incident (vv. 45–46). His high degree of verbal agreement with Mark in what he does report suggests that he did not quote from a separate source but rather abbreviated the Markan account.

An incident on the scale reported by the Markan and Johannine traditions appears highly improbably if Jesus is assumed to have acted alone; it would have had to have been a whirlwind attack that left no opportunity for those who were attacked and for the temple guards to take counteraction. Equally remarkable is the relative calm with which Jesus is reported to have appeared in the temple on the next day (Mark 11:27, //s).

If the followers of Jesus had also been involved in the cleansing of the temple, it could, under the circumstances, have appeared to constitute the beginning of an uprising. There is no suggestion of anything of that kind in either of two traditions. No immediate action was taken against Jesus, although Mark, as we have seen, links the incident to the plot against Jesus by means of 11:18 and 12:12. It is not impossible, of course, to imagine that the arrest of Jesus in Gethsemane followed more immediately, possibly even the same evening, as a direct reaction of the authorities to the temple incident, but we have no evidence on which to base such a conclusion.

By framing the cleansing of the temple with the story of the withered fig tree (Mark 11:12–14, 20–26) Mark appears to indicate metaphorically that the temple had become fruitless and that it was destined for destruction. Matthew treats the story of the withered fig tree as a single incident before the cleansing of the temple (21:18–22), whereas Luke includes it in an independent tradition earlier in his Gospel (13:6–9).

The legendary character of the account of Jesus' entry into Jerusalem and the story's formulation under the influence of the scriptural passage that it was understood to have fulfilled make it impossible to derive from it anything about an actual event in the life of Jesus with reasonable probability. If Jesus' entry was anything like the one described in the account, the conclusion that he had been a messianic pretender would have been inescapable. If, furthermore, the entry had been followed by an incident such as the reported cleansing of the temple, the Jewish leaders would indeed have had every reason to be apprehensive. However, we do not know anything with a sufficient degree of certainty to be able to draw sound conclusions, and almost everything else we know about Jesus tends to contradict an understanding of him as a messianic pretender.

On the other hand, as we have seen, Luke 24:21 and Acts 1:6 provide strong evidence that at least some of his followers did consider Jesus to have been the messiah in a political sense. This is reinforced by the fact that the disciples were armed in Gethsemane. And what if, in conjunction with these political aspirations, an enthusiastic group of Jesus' followers did indeed cheer him at his coming to Jerusalem for the feast with "blessed is he who comes in the name of the Lord; blessed is the coming kingdom of our father David" (Mark 11:10)? Such an incident could certainly have made the Jewish leadership fear that a messianic uprising was brewing.

The close association of incidents such as the entry into Jerusalem and the cleansing of the temple with the grasping of messianic-political power is suggested by the events that occurred in connection with Simon Maccabeus' final consolidation of power, as reported in 1 Maccabees 13:49–53. After the final resistance in the temple fortress was broken "Simon cleansed the fortress of the impurities. Thereupon, on the 23d day of the 2d month of the year 171 [according to the Syrian calendar, 141 B.C.] he took up residence in it with praise and palm branches with [the sound of] cither, cymbal, and harp, and with psalms and hymns, because a great enemy had been driven from Israel" (vv. 50–51). The same incident is reported in 2 Maccabees 10:1–9, with more emphasis on the temple itself: "Maccabeus and those with him, under the guidance of God, took possession of the temple and the city. They razed the altars that had been built by the foreigners in the marketplaces, also in places that had been set aside for that purpose. And after they cleansed the temple they built a new altar, struck fire from stone, and offered a sacrifice after an interruption that had lasted for two years. For eight days with great joy they celebrated a feast in the manner of the feast of booths, remembering how only recently at the time of the feast of booths they lived like wild animals in the mountains and in caves. And so with wreathed wands and blossoming branches, also palm branches, they praised him who had made possible the cleansing of the place that had been sanctified for his sake" (vv. 1–3, 6–7).

These events are not repeated exactly in the story of Jesus' entry into Jerusalem and the cleansing of the temple; many differences are evident. Nevertheless, there are enough similar features to associate the two incidents in which Jesus had reportedly been involved with the grasping of messianic-political power. Comparison with Simon Maccabeus sheds light on the symbolism with which the two incidents are reported in the Jesus tradition. As we will see in the next section, regardless of whether or not Jesus entered regally into Jerusalem and cleansed the temple, the Jewish authorities did fear that he had been involved in an attempt to grasp political-messianic power.

What Jesus himself thought we have no way of knowing with certainty at this point in our inquiry. That he claimed to have been the messiah, the Son of God, the king of the Jews before the Sanhedrin and before Pilate does not necessarily represent historical fact but represents the way early Christianity understood what happened. One would have to concede, however, that if Jesus had allowed his followers to acclaim him as they are presented to have done when he entered Jerusalem, the conclusion would have been unavoidable that he himself had contributed to the impression of a messianic pretender. We cannot know for certain whether this actually happened, but it is important to note that his followers remembered him in this way in the traditions they handed down in early Christianity after his death.

D. THE PREDICAMENT OF THE JEWISH LEADERS (JOHN 11:47–53; #260)

In Mark 14:2, //s we already learned that the Jewish authorities were determined to have Jesus arrested in a way that would avoid a tumult among the people. From our subsequent considerations it became clear that the expectation of a messianic uprising had probably been current in the circles around Jesus. Irrespective of Jesus' potential involvement or noninvolvement in such a movement, John 11:47–53 provides almost certain proof that the Jewish authorities wanted to have him arrested in order to avoid a threatened uprising. It was, of course not the uprising itself that they feared most, but the reprisal from Rome that would have followed. According to verse 48 they were afraid that if Jesus continued doing what he did "all will believe in him, and the Romans will come and destroy both our place and our nation." What the Jewish leaders probably feared was that if the people believed in him as a messiah the resulting messianic uprising would be repressed by Rome with dire consequences for the people.

The decision against Jesus was not taken lightly. It apparently met sufficiently strong opposition to make Caiaphas exclaim with annoyance, "You don't understand anything! You don't consider it better for you if one man dies in the place of the people, and not the whole nation perish!" (vv. 49–50). The evangelist concluded from this that the high priest prophesied Jesus' vicarious death for the people. What evidently happened historically was a tradeoff—in order to prevent the danger of a threatened uprising, the Jewish authorities passed the responsibility for deciding Jesus' fate on to the Romans.

The Jewish authorities sensed that if they arrested Jesus in the presence of the crowds, the potentially volatile situation would have erupted into chaos and turmoil. It was in this regard that Judas's services proved useful. After Jesus had been arrested according to plan, he was first brought to the house of the high priest for interrogation to verify his identity. Once this was done, the Jewish authorities handed him over to the Romans as a messianic pretender, the charge on which Jesus was convicted and executed. Contrary to the Gospel accounts, there appears not to have been a trial before the Sanhedrin. The interrogation of Jesus at the house of the high priest on the night of his arrest was mistaken for a Sanhedrin trial in the tradition.

The Jewish authorities may have made a grave mistake, but if John 11:47–53 reflects the situation, we have reason to believe that they did not act with malice but with concern for the safety of the people. They were in a predicament—either hand over to the Romans someone suspected of being a messianic pretender and accept the risks that that involved, or take responsibility for not having prevented a possible uprising. Since we do not know the facts with certainty we cannot pass judgment on the wisdom of their decision. Even though the Jewish authorities did avoid the dire consequences of a political uprising, did they not in that way become responsible for the very thing that Caiaphas's opposition had feared, the execution of an innocent person?

The tradition of John 11:47–53 provides the last bit of evidence making it possible to piece together the other traditions in a way that provides a probable historical explanation of what happened. The Jewish authorities had Jesus arrested and handed over to the Romans for trial and execution because they feared that his popularity could have led to an uprising, with dire consequences for their people.

Conclusion. Our investigation of the Gospel accounts of Jesus' trial before the Sanhedrin and his execution as a messianic pretender has not answered our question of who Jesus was, although it has given us an indication of what probably took place in the last days of his life. Decisive in the picture that has emerged is that he was crucified because the Roman authorities found him guilty of having been a messianic pretender and that the Jewish authorities initiated the action against him because they feared that the movement they saw gathering around him would lead to an uprising that could have resulted in Roman reprisals of catastrophic proportions. Furthermore, it is clear that the followers of Jesus had been prepared for an armed confrontation when he was arrested in Gethsemane. We have also established that at least some of Jesus' followers considered him a political messiah who was to have liberated Israel from Roman rule. That the disciples were armed in Gethsemane and engaged in a small skirmish with those who had come to arrest Jesus, a skirmish ending in the disciples' flight, provides evidence that makes it difficult to deny with certainty that Jesus may have been involved in a movement of armed resistance against Rome. The tradition concerning the two swords in Luke 22:35–38 is further evidence that his disciples remembered him, even if mistakenly, to have encouraged them to arm themselves.

Summary. We can know little about Jesus with reasonable certainty. Nevertheless, the texts provide enough clues to give us a reasonably defined picture of how Christianity emerged form his activity.

He apparently was the son of a respectable—what one may call middle-class—family in Nazareth. If his father was a cabinetmaker they lived on a relatively comfortable economic level compared with the masses of peasants and day laborers.

About his childhood and youth we know nothing. The legends concerning that time of his life reflect the impression he left on his followers. Legends of his childhood indicate that the significance he had for his followers was not limited to the reporting of historical facts about his life. The limitation of historical facticity comes to vivid expression in the story of his rejection in Nazareth. Those who knew him well historically, rejected him.

At some stage in his life he apparently became a follower of John the Baptist, by whom he was baptized. He did not remain in the circle of John as one of his disciples but returned to Galilee, where we encounter him as a friend of "publicans and sinners" at the height of his activity in the Gospels. However, even after he left the circle of John's followers, he maintained a high regard for John, pointing to him as the one who marked the transition of the ages, from the time before the kingdom of God to the time of its coming (Matt. 11:9–14, //).

The Jesus we encounter in the Gospels espoused a way of life diametrically opposed to that of John. It was a way of life that can be described only as scandalous, as his own statement in reply to the question of John reveals, "Blessed is whoever is not scandalized by me" (Matt. 11:6, //), and as he concedes in the contrast with John, "the Son of Man came eating and drinking, and they called him a glutton and drinker, a friend of publicans and sinners" (Matt. 11:19). Evidence of his scandalous behavior is provided by the confrontation between him and his family in their attempt to persuade him to come home with them (Mark 3:20–21, 32–35, //s), especially in his sharp rejection of their request.

We do not know what motivated Jesus' behavior. A formative influence apparently was the preaching of John the Baptist that the coming of the kingdom of God was imminent. Jesus pointed to John as the decisive eschatological figure whose activity marked the transition from the expectation of the kingdom of God to its arrival. That was the context in which he understood his own activity. The context of the kingdom of God gave a deeply religious meaning to what might otherwise have been a purely personal preference, his association with the religiously and socially underprivileged.

We have substantial evidence that at least some of Jesus' followers thought of him as the messiah who was to liberate Israel from Roman rule, as Acts 1:6 and Luke 24:21 clearly state. That his followers were armed in Gethsemane makes it difficult to deny that he himself may have been involved in armed resistance against Rome. The tradition that he encouraged his disciples to arm themselves (Luke 22:35–38) makes this even more difficult. The stories of his entry into Jerusalem (Mark 11:1–10, //s) and his cleansing of the temple (Mark 11:15–17) contribute further to such an understanding, even if we cannot be sure what lies historically behind those traditions. One might wonder to what degree Jesus' conviction that the activity of John the Baptist marked the beginning of the kingdom of God contributed to these messianic expectations. In any case, whether as a judicial error or with reason, Jesus was condemned to death and executed as a messianic pretender by the Romans. It appears that the Jewish authorities in Jerusalem were involved, not because of vindictiveness, but because they feared that the movement gathering around him could lead to an uprising, which would inevitably have resulted in bloody reprisals from the Romans (John 11:47–53).

The death of a messianic pretender meant the end of the movement that gathered around him. If a messianic movement had clustered around Jesus, it should also have died with his death, as had the movements of every other pretender. The death of Jesus, however, rather than end the significance he had for his followers, gave new life to it by the very fact that they now had to cope with the fact of his death. His death functioned like a filter, allowing to survive only the things about him that remained unaffected by it. At the same time it made of him a symbol for what he represented. That everything did not end with his death in itself indicates that the meaning he had for his followers went beyond that of a mere messianic pretender. They were unable to accept his death as the end of the expectations that had been built up around him. With that we have moved beyond the realm of historical facticity to historical meaning.

The impression that Jesus left with his followers is reflected in the synoptic Gospels' traditions concerning his teaching. Yet we have not a single synoptic saying about which we can say with certainty that it originated from Jesus himself. All sayings reflect the impression that he left with his followers, an impression that grew as Christianity of New Testament times wove the strands of tradition, expanding them as they handed them down. The question of whether a particular saying was actually pronounced by Jesus is not only impossible to answer but, from the point of view of the history of the developing Christian religion, irrelevant. What was important about Jesus for the developing Christian religion was not so much the concrete facts of his life but the impact he had made on his followers, as reflected in the tradition of his life and teachings and in the legends of his birth and childhood. The profoundness of impact sustained Jesus' followers after the shattering experience of his death and enabled them to found a new religion in his name.

In the rest of this book we turn our attention to the nature of the Jesus tradition and how the impression he left with his followers motivated the emergence of the Christian faith. The discussion will be brief, a mere sketch to round off the picture of who Jesus was, to which the main part of this study was devoted. Before we move to the final part, however, we should discuss a passage that stands on the borderline between the life of Jesus and his becoming a symbol for that about him which survived his death, the story of his transfiguration. In the Gospels it appears as a crucial turning point in his life; historically it almost certainly originated as an experience of his enthronement as the Son of God after his resurrection.

CHAPTER 6

The Transfiguration of Jesus
(Mark 9:2–10, //s; #161)

Earlier, in our discussion of Peter's confession (Mark 8:27–33), we mentioned the story of the transfiguration of Jesus as a parallel to Peter's declaration that Jesus was the messiah; the two passages together express the idea that Jesus was the messiah, the Son of God, an understanding that Jesus himself subsequently affirmed in the trial before the Sanhedrin (14:61–62). The story of the transfiguration is a separate tradition which Mark placed in its present position in his Gospel. It breaks into the sequence of 9:1 and 9:11–13. In 9:1 Jesus announces that some of those present will still be alive when the kingdom of God comes, and in verse 11 the disciples respond to that announcement with the question whether it is then correct that, as the scribes say, Elijah has to come first. If one leaves the text as it now stands (vv. 1–13), the disciples would appear to have been puzzled by what Jesus meant with "rising from the dead" (v. 10), but to have asked him an unrelated question about the necessity that Elijah should first return (v. 11). Verse 11 does not make sense after verse 10, revealing that the connection between them is secondary, due to the insertion of verses 2–10 between 1 and 11.

It is not clear why Mark inserted the story of the transfiguration at this point, that is, after Jesus' statement in verse 1 that some of those present would still be alive at coming of the kingdom of God. Does the reference to the future coming of God's kingdom call to mind the messianic secret, which remained concealed from the crowds but was revealed to the disciples at the transfiguration of Jesus? Note in this regard Jesus' statement in 4:11 that the mystery of the kingdom of God remains concealed from others but is revealed to the disciples, "To you the mystery of the kingdom of God is revealed; to those outside everything comes in parables." In the transfiguration story only the three most intimate disciples are initiated into the mystery of the kingdom of God, that is, that Jesus is the Son of God.

Another possible reason why Mark connected the passages could be the appearance of Elijah with Moses in the company of Jesus on the mountain (9:4) and the question about him in verses 11–12. That by itself, however, does not seem to be sufficient motivation for introducing the story of the transfiguration at this point.

The transfiguration itself provides no indication of the time of the incident in the life of Jesus. Mark places it prior to the crucifixion, but nothing in the story itself demands that it be located at that stage of Jesus' life. To the contrary, certain features in the story suggest that it was originally an incident that took place after the resurrection of Jesus. According to the confessional formula in Romans 1:3–4 to which we have referred before, it was through the resurrection from the dead that Jesus became the Son of God: "[Jesus Christ] who was born from the seed of David, by physical descent [literally, "of the flesh"], who was ordained Son of God in power through the resurrection of the dead, by way of the Holy Spirit."

The formula distinguishes explicitly between Jesus' physical descent from David through his birth and his sonship of God through his resurrection from the dead, a second birth through the Holy Spirit. A similar view is expressed in Acts 2:36. At the end of a speech that narrates the facts about the resurrection of Jesus, Peter draws the following conclusion: "Let it therefore be clear to the whole house of Israel that God has made him both Lord and messiah, this Jesus whom you have crucified." The understanding expressed in this statement is that Jesus who had been crucified had since been made Lord and messiah.

By placing the transfiguration of Jesus in its present position in the Gospel, Mark presents Jesus as the Son of God before his crucifixion, but as a mystery that had been revealed only to the most intimate circle of three of his disciples (cf. v. 2). In the present form of the story Jesus is, of course, not made Son of God; it is announced in a revelation to the three disciples that he *is* the Son of God: "This is my son, the beloved one; listen to him" (v. 7). According to Mark, Jesus was already made Son of God at his baptism when a voice from heaven declared, "You are my son, the beloved one; with you I am pleased" (Mark 1:11). As we have seen in connection with the story of Jesus' baptism, these words are a combination of Psalm 2:7, "You are my son; this day I have generated you," and Isaiah 42:1 in a translation that we know only from Matthew 12:18, "Behold, my servant whom I chose; my beloved one with whom my soul is well pleased. I will let my spirit be on him." The words of Psalm 2:7 constitute an oriental formula of adoption with which the enthroned king is adopted as the son of the deity, the way Mark and Luke have it at the baptism of Jesus.

In the present passage the voice from the cloud does not pronounce that Jesus has been appointed the Son of God, as in Mark 1:11, but announces that he is the Son of God. In that regard it is more akin to Isaiah

42:1 than to Psalm 2:7. In the parallel to Mark 1:11, Matthew already says "This is my son, the beloved one" (Matt. 3:17), as in the present verse (Mark 9:7). There is reason to believe that the present passage too was altered into the form of an announcement from the original tradition in which the voice pronounced Jesus the Son of God with the words "you are my son."

It has been suggested—and is widely accepted—that "listen to him" is quoted from Deuteronomy 18:15, where Moses says, "The Lord, your God, will raise for you a prophet like me from your brothers; you will listen to him." The reasons for making this suggestion, however, are not clear. It is not a direct quotation from a known Greek text of Deuteronomy, which reads, "You will listen to him," whereas our verse has "listen to him." On the other hand, it may be an allusion to Isaiah 42:2, which reads in Matthew's version, "He will not argue or cry out, nor will someone hear his voice in the streets" (Matt. 12:19). The Greek term for "hear" and "listen" is the same in both passages. We may conclude that Scripture is alluded to in the words spoken from the cloud and that Isaiah 42:1 and Psalm 2:7 are almost certainly involved but that other allusions remain uncertain.

Mark's version of the story is composite. Verses 9–10 are not an actual part of it but a comment looking back on the incident. As we have indicated in the previous section, these verses express the messianic secret motif, demanding that the mystery that was revealed to the disciples be kept secret until after the resurrection.

Verses 5–6 stand out as a subtheme. They set the disciples who are afraid and uncomprehending apart from Jesus, Moses, and Elijah who are party to the mystery that is being revealed to the disciples. The intention of the booths remains unclear; verse 6 disparages the statement as an expression of Peter's perplexity. Originally, however,it may have had a more substantive meaning, either as an allusion to the feast of the booths or as an expression of the desire to keep Jesus on earth in what may originally have been an enthronement/ascension story. That these verses may be an addition by Mark himself is indicated by Luke's heavy dependence on him here, whereas he appears to have had an independent source for the rest of the story.

A feature of the story probably holding considerable significance is that the cloud out of which the voice came "overshadowed them" (v. 7). In antiquity, a cloud was frequently the means of manifesting the divine presence, specifically in the story of the Exodus from Egypt. It was, however, also the means of making persons disappear, as in Acts 1:9 when Jesus disappeared before the eyes of his disciples. In Homer the gods frequently used haze (literally, "thick air") to remove persons from the scene (for example, *Iliad* 3.380–81; 20.444; *Odyssey* 7.15). In our passage the divine presence is clearly revealed by the voice from the cloud, but that the cloud "overshadowed them" suggests that it also functioned to remove, not only Moses and Elijah, but Jesus as well from the scene in what was originally an ascension/enthronement story. If verses 5–6 were a later addition, with verse 7 originally following on 4, the statement that the cloud "overshadowed them" would have referred specifically to Jesus, Moses, and Elijah.

Textual clues indicate strongly, therefore, that the transfiguration on the mountain was originally an ascension/enthronement story, calling to mind the second part of the hymn in Philippians, "Therefore God exalted him and granted him the name which is above every name, that in the name of Jesus every knee of those in heaven and those on earth and those under the earth will bow down, and every tongue will confess that Jesus Christ is Lord, to the glory of God, the father" (Phil. 2:9–11). The story of the transfiguration tells how Jesus was transfigured on the mountain of the ascension (cf. Matt. 28:16) in the presence of his disciples and was then taken up into heaven, disappearing in a cloud before their eyes. This scene resembles Acts 1:9 "And as he was saying this, with [the disciples] looking on, he was raised up, and a cloud took him away from their eyes." It is an enthronement scene; the two persons accompanying Jesus, secondarily identified as Moses and Elijah, represent his royal entourage, and the voice from the cloud pronounces the words of installation.

Since he placed this incident in the life of Jesus, Mark was not able to leave the statement that "suddenly, looking around, [the disciples] saw no one" (v. 8a) unqualified. He added "except Jesus alone with them" (v. 8b), which made it possible for him to have Jesus descend from the mountain with his disciples and continue his activity on earth (vv. 9–10).

Only three disciples were present at the transfiguration, Peter, James, and John (v. 2). In the original tradition this probably meant the three "pillars" of the church in Jerusalem to whom Paul refers in Galatians 2:9, James being the brother of Jesus, not James the son of Zebedee, the brother of John (cf. Mark 1:9; 3:17, //s). This group of the three intimates who formed the innermost circle around Jesus (cf. also Mark 5:37, 14:33, //s) is probably a projection back into the life of Jesus of the tradition of the three pillars in Jerusalem. James the son of Zebedee takes the place of "the brother of the Lord" in the Gospels, since tradition remembers that the brothers of Jesus were not positively disposed towards him (cf. Mark 3:21, and especially John 7:5).

The statement that the incident occurred "after six days" (v. 2) is related to the subsequent celebration in the early church of January 6 as the day of the epiphany. The question is from what day it was calculated; in an early form of the tradition it may have been either the day of the crucifixion or of the resurrection, but now it is from the beginning of the year.

As has already been mentioned, Luke primarily used an independent source for his version of the story, except for the account of Peter's suggestion about the booths where he shows heavy verbal dependence on Mark (cf. Mark 9:5–6, //s). Luke added a scene about the disciples' sleepiness (vv. 31–32), which does not fit well with Peter's suggestion about the booths in verse 33. It should be noted that in this independent tradition Luke refers to "the two men" who were with Jesus (v. 32) as if they had not been identified in verse 30. This provides additional support for the presumption that they were not identified as Moses and Elijah in the original tradition and suggests that Luke's identification of them in verse 30 may have been influenced by Mark. Furthermore, Luke has "some eight days" (v. 28) in the place of Mark's "after six days." He also provides an additional indication that the formulation of the voice from the cloud recalled Isaiah 42:1. In place of Mark's "the beloved one" he had "the elect one," drawing from a different Greek translation of the passage from Isaiah. In contrast with Matthew's version in 12:18, which has "my beloved one," the Septuagint reads "my elect one."

Matthew follows Mark rather closely, except that, typically, he leaves out the statement of Mark 9:6 that Peter did not know what to say because he was afraid. After the voice had spoken from the cloud Matthew pictures the disciples in a posture of awed worship, with Jesus reassuring them (Matt. 17:6–7).

Conclusion. The story of Jesus' transfiguration already places us in the time after the resurrection of Jesus, even though it is recorded in the Gospels in the time of his life on earth. It is our task now to investigate how the belief in his resurrection originated and how the Christian religion emerged from the events of Jesus' life and his death on the cross.

Part 2

___

FROM JESUS TO PRIMITIVE CHRISTIANITY

So, Madame, it is not to them [the two distinguished men who loved you], but to love itself that you give recognition. They were merely love's interpreters.

GUY DE MAUPASSANT

Introduction

In the first part of this study we tried to determine what could be known about Jesus from the information provided by the synoptic Gospels, supplemented occasionally by information from the Fourth Gospel. In this second part we will try to round off the picture we obtained of Jesus by noting the way in which he determined the development of the Christian religion. We have already seen that Christianity did not develop immediately from the activity of Jesus but resulted from the attempts of his followers to cope with his death. The determining factor in these attempts, and their fundamental motivation, was the impression Jesus left with those who knew him, an impression that had more power than could be registered in terms of the mere facts of his life. One might say that Jesus grew on them during his lifetime but even more so after his death.

This second part of the study contains two chapters. In chapter 7 we will look at the way in which Scripture may have helped the followers of Jesus cope with his death and so begin the process from which primitive Christianity emerged. It will concern basically Acts 2:24–31, supplemented by a consideration of parts of Luke 24:13–27.

In chapter 8 we will first try to understand the way in which the tradition of the teaching of Jesus developed as it was handed down in New Testament Christianity. This will be done by investigating two types of tradition, beatitudes and parables. Discussion of beatitudes will focus on the beatitudes in Matthew's Sermon on the Mount (Matt. 5:3–12) and the beatitudes and woes of Luke's Sermon on the Plain (Luke 6:20–26). The investigation of parables will be limited to certain statements in Mark 4 that reveal a variety of conceptions of the parables, supplemented by the study of a single parable, that of the banquet (Matt. 22:1–4, //).

Finally, we will note how in the description of the last judgment (Matt. 25:31–46), New Testament Christianity moved toward locating the meaning of Jesus beyond the confines of a mere confession of him as the Christ. In this passage the confession of Jesus is interpreted in terms of a concern for humanity in need similar to the concern that had motivated Jesus himself. In this way Christianity reaffirmed its ground in the activity of Jesus.

CHAPTER 7

The Emergence of the Christian Faith

How did the transition take place from the movement that had developed around Jesus during his life to the Christian religion that emerged after his death? The movement that had gathered around Jesus was itself not yet the subsequent Christian religion, even though Christianity was rooted in it. The Jesus movement apparently was a complex movement with strongly divergent elements, ranging from the socially and religiously disinherited who gathered around Jesus because he accepted them, through apocalyptically oriented followers who believed his claim that the kingdom of God had already come, to political messianic groups who saw in him the messiah whom they expected to liberate Israel from Roman rule. All of these were views in which Jesus himself may have participated.

What emerged after the death of Jesus included something of all of these but in no case represented a simple continuation of any of them. Christianity at the time of the New Testament did not understand itself as religiously disinherited but rather developed considerable religious self-esteem; nor did it understand the kingdom of God as already present but expected its coming in the near future when Jesus returned as the Son of Man. As we have seen, Jesus' followers, unlike Jesus himself, did not understand John, but Jesus, as the decisive eschatological figure whose activity signaled the coming of the kingdom of God, at the same time shifting the time of the kingdom's coming from the past, inaugurated by the activity of John the Baptist, to the future, with the expected return of Jesus as the Son of Man. And early Christianity certainly did not understand Jesus to have intended armed revolt against the Romans, even though *messiah* remained the basic christological title, until it became just another name for him in its Greek form, *christos*.

It is neither possible, nor is it the intention here, to render a complete account of how Christianity emerged from the movement around Jesus after his death. All we will do is to focus on the crucial period immediately after his death and to note how a single factor, namely, Scripture, may have contributed to the first steps in the crucial transition from the despair experienced by Jesus' followers at his death to the beginning of a new understanding of him. The clue to the way in which Scripture influenced their thinking may be found in Acts 2:24–29. At a fundamental level, the emergence of Christianity meant a shift of focus from what Jesus did and said to the person of Jesus himself, but this did not exclude incorporating some of what Jesus taught into belief in his person. However, one development brought the interpretation of the meaning of faith in Jesus full circle back to the beginning, by refocusing on behavior similar to that of Jesus himself in the description of the last judgment (Matt. 25:31–46).

THE DEATH AND RESURRECTION OF JESUS (ACTS 2:24–29; LUKE 24:13–27)

According to Mark, Jesus' followers fled after he was taken into custody in Gethsemane (Mark 14:50, //). Peter is reported to have made a feeble, disheartened attempt to stay in touch with the further developments (Mark 14:66–72, //s; also John 18:25–27). Women are recorded as the only ones present at the scene of his crucifixion (Mark 15:40–41, //s); only John reports that the beloved disciple was there too (19:26–27). According to tradition, it was the women who went to the grave on that Sunday morning and discovered that Jesus had risen (Mark 16:1–8, //s; cf. Luke 24:22–24), and to whom he first appeared (Mark 16:9–11, //s). In what appears to have been the more normative tradition, however, Jesus' subsequent appearance to Peter was given priority over this appearance to the women (cf. 1 Cor. 15:5; Luke 24:34).

With the death of Jesus the movement that had gathered around him appears to have come to an end, a point that is made by the story of the two disciples on their way to Emmaus. Note especially their statement to the unrecognized Jesus, "We believed that he was the one who was to have redeemed Israel, but now with all of this it is already the third day since this happened" (Luke 24:21). As soon as the two disciples recognize that Jesus is alive, they immediately return to Jerusalem (v. 33). It was, so to speak, from the ashes of the Jesus movement that Christianity was born—a resurrection from the dead, not a mere continuation of the life that preceded his death. As Jesus' response to the despondent Emmaus disciples reveals, Scripture may have played an important part in this transition from death to a new life. "And he said to them, 'Oh you who are so uncomprehending and heavy-hearted not to believe in everything the prophets said. Did the messiah not have to suffer and so enter into his glory' And beginning from Moses and from all the prophets he interpreted for them in all the Scriptures the matters concerning himself" (vv. 25–27).

That the messiah had to die and so enter into his glory was not evident in the Scriptures. This must have been a discovery that the followers of Jesus made after his death. It is worth noting that here too the disclosure is remembered not as having been made by Jesus during his life, but by the resurrected Christ. A clue as to how this discovery was made may be found in the quotation of Psalm 16:8–11 in the speech of Peter in Acts 2 and in two comments that frame the quotation (Acts 2:24 and 29).

The reader should note in connection with the discussion below that there is an incongruity between the Hebrew, Greek, and RSV texts' enumeration of Psalms 16 and 18. These two psalms are numbered differently in the Septuagint, namely, 15 and 17, respectively. Verse enumerations remain the same in the Hebrew and the Greek. In the RSV, however, the verse enumeration of Psalm 18 is different. So, for example, the two verses that are referred to below are numbered 4 and 5 in the RSV but are 5 and 6 in the Hebrew and Greek texts. In order to simplify the discussion below, references will be to the RSV enumeration because I assume that is the text that most readers will use. Those who want to use the Hebrew and Greek should bear these incongruencies in mind.

Peter's speech in Acts 2 presupposes that the resurrection of Jesus had already taken place, that he had appeared to his disciples on more than one occasion, and that he had ascended into heaven. The quotation of Psalm 16 in the speech is thus a comment on the fact of the resurrection. The speech looks back on the event, and Psalm 16 is quoted as it scriptural confirmation. Some clues indicate however, that the psalm did not originally function as a comment on the resurrection but as an assurance to the followers of Jesus that the messiah had to die in order to enter into his glory. It is an assurance similar to Jesus' statement to the Emmaus disciples in Luke 24:26.

The psalm does not address circumstances in which the threat of death had already been overcome but rather expresses confidence in a safe outcome of a mortally dangerous situation: "My flesh too will yet dwell in hope, because you will not abandon my soul to Hades, nor will you allow your holy one to see corruption" (Acts 2:26–27). It is a literal quotation from the Septuagint of Psalm 15:9c–10. The Hebrew reads differently, "My flesh also dwells secure, because you will not abandon my soul to Sheol; you will not let your devout one see the grave."

This difference is of considerable significance in view of the comment that follows the quotation of the psalm in Acts 2:29, "Brothers, it is possible to say to you quite frankly concerning the patriarch David, that he both died and was buried, and his grave is with us to this day." The point of the comment is that in the psalm David speaks not for himself, but for the messiah, because his death reveals that his statement could not apply to himself. In verse 10 of the psalm he says that God's devout one will not see the grave, but David himself did die and was buried. Peter's comment concludes with "and his grave is with us to this day" to emphasize the point. Thus, the statement that God's devout one would not see the grave is taken to apply to the messiah who would not die and be buried.

It should be noted that Peter's comment is not applicable in the same way to the Greek text in which the reference is not to not seeing the grave, but to not seeing corruption. Even though the Greek is quoted in our passage the comment obviously presupposes the Hebrew text of the psalm. We must assume that the passage was originally formulated in Aramaic, the Semitic language that was spoken in Palestine at the time, and that when it was translated into Greek, the quotation from the psalm was not retranslated but simply taken from the existing Septuagint translation.

A difficulty that arises in connection with Peter's comment as it relates to Jesus is that he too died and was buried. This is explicitly stated in one of the oldest known confessional formulas, the one quoted by Paul in 1 Corinthians 15, which reads in part, "That Christ died for our sins . . ., and that he was buried" (vv. 3–4). Thus, what makes the psalm inapplicable to David makes it equally inapplicable to Jesus, and yet it is assumed that it does apply to him, notably, however, emphasizing his resurrection and ignoring his death and burial.

Three possible explanations can be given for this contradiction: (1) The author of the comment was inattentive and did not recognize that what made the psalm inapplicable to David made it equally inapplicable to Jesus. (2) It was assumed that Jesus had ascended to heaven immediately after he died, as his words to one of the criminals who was crucified with him suggest, "This day you will be with me in paradise" (Luke 23:43). Even then the comment would still not fit perfectly, but the author may have been aware of that and tried to cope with the problem by adding that David's "grave is with us to this day." (3) The comment was not formulated with Jesus in mind but expressed an earlier expectation that the messiah, whoever he might be, would never die, as expressed, for example, in the words of the angel of the annunciation, "He will reign over the house of Israel in eternity, and to his kingdom there will be no end" (Luke 1:33). The same conviction is behind the despair expressed by the Ammaus disciples when they say, "It is now the third day since these things happened" (Luke 24:21). Since Jesus too had died and been buried, their hope that he was the messiah was shattered. Of these three explanations, only the last one fits logically, but then, in literature of this kind, logical consistency is not always of primary significance.

What may help in solving this difficulty is the comment that precedes the quotation of Psalm 16 in Peter's speech. The comment reads, "Whom God raised, untying the pangs of death, because they were incapable of overpowering him" (Acts 2:24). The formulation is unusual; one does not usually speak of "untying" pangs or pain but ropes or cords. This difficulty is solved by the following considerations. The phrase "pangs of death" appears to have been taken from another messianic psalm, Psalm 18:4, which reads in the Septuagint, "The pangs of death encompassed me." The Hebrew, however, reads "The cords [or "ropes" or "lines"] of death encompassed me." That may explain the strange formulation "untying the pangs of death," which probably read in the original Hebrew/ Aramaic formulation, "untying the cords of death." This comment too appears to presuppose the Hebrew text. It brought to expression the understanding that although Jesus died, the cords of death that encompassed him (Psalm 18:4) did not remain tied. When the comment was translated into Greek, the existing Septuagint translation of the psalm was again used, resulting in the unusual formulation "untying the pangs of death."

One may ask why the Hebrew term for "cords, ropes, or lines" could be translated with the Greek word for "pangs or pains." The reason is that in the plural, the Hebrew term (ḥblym) for both of these meanings is indistinguishable. (Actually the same would be true for the singular [ḥbl] in the unvocalized Hebrew text that was used at the time.) In Psalm 18:4 "the pangs of death" makes good sense as a translation of the Hebrew "cords of death," even though the formulation is somewhat unusual, "The pangs of death encompass me." It expresses the painful threat of death. The same applies to the translation of "the cords of Sheol entangled me" in the Hebrew of Psalm 18:5 with "the pangs of Sheol encircled me" in the Greek. Only the formulation "untying of the pangs" in our passage is strange, but now we have an idea of how it could have come about.

A new question is what the reference to "the cords of death" in Psalm 18:4 (Acts 2:24) has to do with the quotation of Psalm 16:8–11 in verses 25–28. The quotation of the psalm obviously clarifies the comments in verse 24, which refers to Psalm 18. This is indicated by the introduction to the quotation, "For David says concerning him . . ." (v. 25). In Psalm 18 it is stated that "the cords of death encompassed me" (v. 4) and "the cords of Sheol entangled me" (v. 5), which originally referred to mortal danger, not to actual death. The two statements could, however, also be read in this second sense, as referring to being actually dead and in Sheol. This is obviously the way in which they are understood in verse 24 of our passage, according to which the "cords [or 'pangs'] of death" that already encompassed Jesus were untied.

Psalm 16 is then understood as furnishing proof for this, most clearly when the psalmist, speaking for the messiah, says, "You will not abandon my soul to Sheol" (Acts 2:27, Psalm 16:10). Although the cords of Sheol already encompassed the messiah, God did not abandon him to Sheol but untied the cords, which were therefore unable to hold him (Acts 2:24).

The connection between these two psalms was discovered by the followers of Jesus through the presence of the Hebrew term for "cords, lines" in both of them. Psalm 16:6 reads, "The cords [or "lines"] fell in excellent places for me." In Jewish interpretation the presence of the same term in two biblical passages suggested a connection between them. That such a connection was assumed between Psalms 16 and 18 is made certain by the fact that Acts 2:24, which refers to Psalm 18:4, is explained by the quotation of Psalm 16:8–11. The cords of death, which encompassed the messiah according to Psalm 18:4, fell in excellent places for him according to Psalm 16:6, that is, they were untied. As the rest of Psalm 16 indicates, death was not able to overpower him. According to these verses the messiah saw God continually before him, strengthening his right hand so that he should not waver. His heart was glad and his soul rejoiced. He felt secure in his flesh because he knew that God would not abandon him to Sheol nor let him see the grave, that he would show him the path to life, and that there was fullness of joy in God's presence and pleasure at his right hand forever (Psalm 16:8–1, cf. Acts 2:25–28). To put it succinctly, "The messiah had to die and so enter into his glory" (Luke 24:26).

The quotation of Psalm 16:8–11 in Peter's speech in Acts and the two comments that frame it (vv. 24 and 29) reveal three distinct interpretations of the psalm. (1) The earliest comes to expression in the comment in verse 29, which interprets it as proof that the messiah, in contrast with David, would not die. This interpretation is pre-Christian, since it could not have originated after Jesus' death and burial. It could have existed in those circles of Jesus' followers who had messianic expectations of him before his death. (2) The second interpretation takes Psalm 18:5 and 6 as references to the death of the messiah and understands Psalm 16:8–11 as the expression of confidence that death would not overpower him, that he would not be abandoned in Sheol. This interpretation appears to have originated among the followers of Jesus after his death. The connection between the two psalms made them confident that despite his death, Jesus was the messiah. (3) The third interpretation is that found in the present text. It no longer struggles with the problem of the death of the messiah, because it already looks back on the fact of his resurrection and takes Psalm 16:8–11 as an interpretation of that fact. In this context the comment in verse 24 no longer looks forward with confidence that the messiah would not be overcome by the cords of death that encompassed him, but looks back to the resurrection as an accomplished fact.

Acts 2:24–29 shows that Scripture played an important role in helping the followers of Jesus cope with the fact of his death. Through Scripture, specifically the connection between Psalms 16 and 18, they came to the recognition that his death was not the end, that through his death he entered into his glory. In their attempts to cope with the shattering experience of his death, Jesus' followers read Psalm 18 as an affirmation that the messiah was expected to die, and through the association established between Psalms 16 and 18 by the Hebrew word for "cords" they understood Psalm 16 to say that God would not abandon the messiah in Sheol. Psalm 18 therefore predicted Jesus' death, and Psalm 16 that he would not remain in the realm of death.

Psalm 16 already spoke of the messiah seeing God constantly before him (v. 8) and of the fullness of joy he experienced in God's presence (v. 11). It revealed that the messiah was with God. Other messianic passages filled out the picture, particularly Psalm 110:1, "The Lord said to my lord, 'Sit at my right hand until I have made your enemies a footstool under your feet' " (Acts 2:34; Mark 12:36, //s; 14:62, //s; 1 Cor. 15:25; Heb. 1:8, and frequently alluded to elsewhere). These images led to a fundamental reconceptualization of the messiahship of Jesus and also of the designation *messiah* itself. Jesus could no longer be conceived of as the one who was to liberate Israel (as in Luke 24:21 and Acts 1:6) because through death he had entered his glory (Luke 24:26) and now sat (or stood) at the right hand of God (cf. Acts 7:56).

With Jesus in heaven the kingdom of God could also no longer be conceived of as already present, because his life ended with the catastrophe of his death, not with the coming of the kingdom. But it now became possible to recognize in him the Son of Man who, according to Daniel 7:13, proceeded on the clouds of heaven to "the ancient of days" and was presented before him, an image in agreement with what was said in Psalm 110:1. In due course, however, he was no longer understood as proceeding to God but returning to earth on the clouds of heaven (Mark 14:62, //s). It is important to note in this connection that the fourth evangelist denies that Jesus was expected to act as a judge (John 3:17).

The attention now increasingly shifted from the teaching and activity of Jesus to his person. A decisive criterion for the future judgment by the Son of Man became loyalty to Jesus: "Everyone who acknowledges me before people, the son of Man will acknowledge before the angels of God, but whoever denies me before people will be denied before the angels of God" (Luke 12:8).

Many other factors contributed to the development of primitive Christianity. Of decisive importance were the appearances of the resurrected Jesus (cf. 1 Cor. 15:5–8; Luke 24:34; Mark 16:9–11, //s, etc.). They made the reality of the resurrection more concrete and so became the foundation for the belief in it. This is the situation that we have in the interpretation of Psalm 16 in Acts 2:24–29. Scripture no longer provided primary evidence for the resurrection but confirmed it, as Paul writes in 1 Corinthians, "That he was raised on the third day according to the Scriptures, and that he appeared to Peter, then to the twelve; after that he appeared to five hundred brothers together, of whom the majority are still around, but of whom some have died; after that he appeared to James, then to all the apostles; and last of all, as if to one born prematurely, he appeared also to me" (15:5–8). The resurrection is in accord with Scripture, but it is known through the appearances of the risen Christ. Paul appeals to the appearances as confirmation that Christ was raised. In Luke 24:25–27 the risen Christ appealed to Scripture to reassure his disciples that it was through death that he entered his glory.

In these early phases of primitive Christianity the focus was on the expectation of the return of Jesus as Son of Man, coordinated with the tradition of his life on earth. The purely eschatological conception in Daniel 7:13 of someone like a son of a man proceeding to the presence of God was applied to the earthly existence of Jesus as well. Jesus was not referred to as the Son of Man with regard to his earthly activity in sayings such as "the Son of Man came eating and drinking, and they said, 'Look a man who is a glutton and a drinker, a friend of publicans and sinners'" (Matt. 1:29, //s). At this stage his death had not yet achieved significance in itself. It was merely the transition from his earthly to his heavenly existence, as in Luke 24:26, "The messiah must die and so enter into his glory."

As Christianity expanded beyond the limits of a Jewish sect (cf. Acts 24:5, 14; 28:22) non-Jewish ideas also became factors in its development. In particular, the conception of the dying and rising cult deity of the mystery religions provided the young religion with the means of positively interpreting the death of Jesus as God's redemptive act into which the believer was initiated through baptism (cf. particularly Rom. 6:3–5). Christianity, nevertheless, did not become just another mystery religion, because the older conceptions continued alongside the new ones and were incorporated into them. Jesus' dying and rising was conceived of as the suffering and rising of the Son of Man (Mark 8:31; 9:31; and 10:33–34, //s)). In this way the entire complex of ideas that had already developed concerning him as the Son of Man merged with the conception of his dying and rising. Under the influence of scriptural passages such as Isaiah 53:4–5 (cf. Matt. 8:17) his death came to be conceived of as vicarious, as stated in the confessional formula quoted by Paul in 1 Corinthians 15, "That Christ died for our sins according to the Scriptures" (v. 3).

A development that became the fundamental point of conflict between Jews and the young religion was that although grounded in Judaism, Christianity came to understand Jesus as Son of God in ways that were blasphemous to Jews, as we noted in our discussion of Jesus' trial before the Sanhedrin, and specifically John 10:30–36. Under the influence of non-Jewish thinking Jesus was understood to have been either divinely generated (Luke 1:35; Matt. 1:20), or to have preexisted as a divine being in heaven (Phil. 2:6–7, cf. Col. 2:9; John 1:1–5). Not only was this conception blasphemous to the Jews; it probably also presented many Jewish Christians with a serious predicament of how to maintain their monotheistic faith and Christian belief in Jesus as the Son of God at the same time.

In the development of New Testament Christianity into a religion of salvation through faith in Christ the tradition of the teachings of Jesus and of his association with the socially and religiously deprived was not abandoned but became subservient to faith in him as the Savior. The acknowledgment of him became the fundamental criterion on which persons were to be judged, as the saying in Luke 12:8–9, //s reveals. Opposition against Christianity, and particularly persecution of it, reinforced the call for perseverance in the faith in Jesus as an expression of loyalty to what he represented. This is what the final beatitude in Matthew and Luke calls for: "Blessed are you when they despise you and persecute you and speak falsely every evil against you for my sake. Rejoice and be glad, for your reward will be great in heaven" (Matt. 5:11–12, //). Faith in Christ became *the* way of expressing and living out loyalty to what he represented. There was a danger in this development. In the emphasis on faith in Christ, what Jesus represented could recede into the background to such a degree that it lost all significance. That this danger was real is shown by Matthew when he warns in 7:21, "Not everyone who calls me Lord, Lord, will enter into the kingdom of the heavens, but the person who does the will of my father who is in the heavens."

Inasmuch as the focus in the emergence of primitive Christianity first shifted from the behavior of Jesus to his person, from *discipleship of* him to *faith in* him, one could consider the movement of Christianity to have gone full circle back to its origins when faith in Christ was in turn interpreted by behavior similar to that of Jesus. We see this return to its source in Matthew 25:31–46, the final passage we want to discuss in this study. But before we move to that discussion it will be worth considering how the traditions of Jesus' teachings were handed down and adapted to new situations in the developing Christian religion. We cannot be sure which of the traditions concerning Jesus' teaching originated from Jesus himself, but from the way they are presented in the Gospels we are able to uncover how New Testament Christians reacted to these traditions as they handed them down. We will follow this development by focusing on the beatitudes and the parables.

CHAPTER 8

The Jesus Tradition

In this final chapter we will take note of the way in which the Jesus tradition was handed down and developed further in New Testament Christianity: the beatitudes (Matt. 5:3–12, //), the parables (Mark 4:9–20, 33–34, //s), focusing on the Parable of the Banquet (Matt. 22:1–14, //), and the description of the last judgment (Matt. 25:31–46).

A. THE BEATITUDES (MATT. 5:3–12, //s, #51)

Matthew's so-called Sermon on the Mount is not a sermon at all but a series of individual sayings, probably collected by Matthew himself, some of it thematically, e.g., the antitheses (Matt. 5:31–48). A number of these sayings appear in different versions in other locations in Mark and Luke, notably in Luke's briefer, so-called Sermon on the Plain (Luke 6:20–49).

Matthew introduces the sermon by having Jesus ascend the mountain to give his instruction (5:1–2). It is reminiscent of Moses ascending Mount Sinai to receive the Law from God. Jesus is presented as the new Moses who ascends the mountain to give the final interpretation of the Law. Matthew's introduction has a parallel in Luke's introduction to the Sermon on the Plain (Luke 6:20a), but with no allusion to Moses and Mount Sinai. Both introductions are followed by the beatitudes. In both case, thus, the beatitudes provide the context within which Jesus' instruction is to be understood.

Luke includes fairly close parallels for three of Matthew's beatitudes: Matthew's first (v. 3), fourth (v. 6), and last (vv. 11–12) are paralleled by Luke's first (v. 20b), second (v. 21a), and last (vv. 22–23). Furthermore, although Luke has no parallel for Matthew's second beatitude, "Blessed are those that mourn, for they will be comforted" (v. 4), there is a suggestion of a parallel in the additional term *mourn* in his third woe, which is coordinate with this third beatitude. Luke's third beatitude reads, "Blessed are those who weep now, for you will laugh" (v. 21b); the coordinate woe reads, "Woe to those who laugh now, for you will *mourn* and weep" (v. 25b). The added *mourn* suggests a woe that presupposes a beatitude such as Matthew's second. It will be noted that Luke's first three woes are exact inversions of his first three beatitudes, except for this additional term.

One of the distinctive features of Luke's beatitudes is their coordination with a woe in each case. Luke's beatitudes, furthermore, are in the second person, whereas Matthew's, except the last one, are all in the third person.

The final beatitude in both Matthew and in Luke is more extensive and is clearly addressed to the Christian community experiencing persecution, whereas the others speak more generally of the poor, those that mourn, and so forth. Verbal similarities in the two versions of the final beatitude are limited. It is nevertheless evident that both versions are parallel forms of a single beatitude that was a product of the early Christian community, probably pronounced by an early Christian prophet as a saying of the living Lord Jesus Christ. A similar blessing and curse, although not in the beatitude and woe form, can be found in Luke 12:8–9, //: "Let me tell you, everyone who acknowledges me before people, him will the Son of Man also acknowledge before the angels of God, but he who renounces me before people will be denounced before the angels of God" (cf. Mark 8:38, //, which has the blessing form only).

The Lukan form of the beatitudes—in the second person and accompanied by coordinate woes—is formulated in conformity with the blessing and curse formula of early prophets, found in Luke 12:8–9, //, quoted above. The Matthean version of the beatitudes, except for the final one, is in the third person and thus more indirect. The third person form may be the more original. It is difficult to understand how Matthew might have altered the more personal second person form to the remote third person when the intention of his Gospel, as is the case with the others, was to address his readers. Furthermore, if he altered the first eight into the third person, why would he have left the final beatitude in the second person?

The Matthean and Lukan versions express concerns that are distinctive to each of the two evangelists. Matthew's concern for proper moral behavior comes to expression in the blessings pronounced on persons who have commendable moral qualities, whereas Luke's concern for the religiously and socially underprivileged finds expression in the blessing of persons who are deprived. Furthermore, the repeated "now" in Luke's second and third beatitudes and woes (vv. 21 and 25) emphasizes his understanding that the reversal of circumstances brought about by the coming of the kingdom of God was still future. Luke had given up the expectation of an imminent parousia of Christ and thus the imminent coming of the kingdom of God.

Matthew's "poor *in spirit*" and "those that hunger and thirst *for righteous-*

ness" in his first and fourth beatitudes may be additions by means of which he or his tradition clarified that the poverty and hunger did not refer to socioeconomic conditions but to the moral qualities of the persons concerned. Similar moral qualities are presupposed in the rest of his beatitudes, except for the second one. The second beatitude is based on Isaiah 61:2, which is part of the scriptural passage to which Jesus appealed in his reply to the question of John the Baptist (Matt. 11:5, //): "He sent me to proclaim good tidings to the poor, to heal the brokenhearted, . . . to console [or "to comfort"—the same Greek work is used] all those that mourn" (Is. 61:1–2). Note that the first beatitude, if one excludes the added "in spirit" of the Matthean version, is an allusion to the first verse of the Isaiah passage. While this clearly establishes the influence of Isaiah 61:1–2 on the formulation of the beatitudes, it also shows that the moral qualifications in Matthew's first and fourth beatitudes may indeed be secondary. Matthew's third beatitude (v. 5) is based on Psalm 37:11, and his sixth (v. 8) is an allusion to Psalm 24:4.

In the beatitudes, as in a kaleidoscope with ever-changing figures, we can see a variety of images produced by the interweaving and expanding of the Jesus tradition in New Testament Christianity. It is possible to discern earlier and later layers in this process of handing down the tradition. The idea of such discernment never occurred to New Testament Christians. They undoubtedly felt the influence of Jesus as strongly in the later formulations as in the earlier ones. New Testament Christianity was not an orthodoxy, concerned with the tradition of historically pure sayings of Jesus. His influence was a dynamic power, which generated new formulations, expressing new understandings in far greater variety than would have been possible in his brief lifetime. The significance of Jesus cannot be limited to that life alone; it was effective in ever new ways in the development of a dynamic, growing religion which began during his lifetime and continued throughout the centuries to the present. That the development of the Christian religion also includes perversions is a price that had to be paid for having a living religion rather than a lifeless orthodoxy. There is thus more usefulness in the discrimination of layers of tradition than the futile attempt to distinguish a single original layer. The unraveling of layers of tradition helps us grasp something of the dynamic power with which the influence of Jesus manifested itself in the lives of New Testament Christians as they collected, expanded, reformulated, and added to his sayings in the process of handing them down.

The earliest layer of the beatitudes is probably represented by beatitudes that simply pronounce the blessedness of the underprivileged—the poor, those who mourn, those who are hungry—because with the coming of the kingdom of God their situations would be reversed. These beatitudes, as we have seen, express an understanding similar to that of Jesus' reply to the question of John in Matthew 11:5–6, when he announced that the predictions of Isaiah 61:1–2 were being fulfilled. The same passage is recalled in Matthew's first and second beatitudes and in Luke's first. This earliest layer is most clearly represented by Matthew's first, second, and fourth beatitudes (without the added moral connotations of the first and fourth) and by Luke's first and second.

The latest layer of the beatitudes is represented by the final beatitude in Matthew and in Luke. It is clearly a product of the New Testament Christian community as it experienced persecution.

The middle layer contains those beatitudes that adapt the earliest formulations to new situations, for example, Matthew's additions in his first and second beatitudes, which emphasize the importance of virtue, as well as new beatitudes in a similar moralizing vein, such as Matthew's third and fifth through eighth. Changes in the Lukan tradition are less pronounced. One such change, however, is the "now" added in his second and third beatitudes and woes, reflecting his understanding that the expected reversal that was to be accomplished by the parousia of Christ still lay in the future.

And so, not only in the earliest, but in all of these layers in the tradition of the beatitudes the influence of Jesus manifested itself in New Testament Christianity, addressing continually changing situations. A similar situation can be discerned in connection with the parables, where even greater changes took place in the transmission of tradition.

B. THE PARABLES

The parables of Jesus are the most colorful of his sayings. The reason is evident—they are stories that have an appeal of their own, irrespective of what is meant by them. Indeed, the parables have endured the most radical changes in meaning of all the sayings of Jesus. It is possible that there was a time when they were understood, not to have conveyed, but to have concealed meaning, as we will see in the discussion of the layers of tradition in Mark 4, //s. Nevertheless, the parables were not merely handed down as interesting stories told by Jesus. As the parable of the great feast in Matthew 22:1–14, // reveals, they too were adapted to express new meanings for the changing situations in which New testament Christians found themselves.

1. THE MEANING OF THE PARABLES (MARK 4:9–20, 33–34, //s; #122–24, 130)

The material collected in Mark 4 contains more than one conception of what a parable means. It represents different layers in the tradition, reflecting the struggle of New Testament Christians to understand the parables.

A first conception is suggested by the concluding remark of the parable of the sower, "Whoever has ears to hear, let him/her hear" (Mark 4:9, //s). Once the parable has been told, the hearer is left to recognize its meaning. No explanation is to be expected, because, as an illustration of a point that is being made, a parable is itself an explanation. The same saying, or variants of it, is frequently used in different contexts in the Gospels, essentially with the same meaning. (Cf. Mark 4:23; Matt. 11:5; 13:43; Luke 14:35, also in other places in some manuscripts, as well as in Revelation, for example, 2:7, 11, 17, etc., and in the **Gospel of Thomas**).

In the parallel versions of the saying of Mark 4:9, Matthew and Luke agree partly with each other against Mark, and Luke partly agrees with Mark against Matthew. Luke's agreement with Mark is discernible in the RSV translation; both have "ears to hear." The agreement between Matthew and Luke, however, is not brought out in the translation, which reads literally, "The one having ears" against Mark's "whoever has ears." This rather complicated relationship between the three evangelists will be encountered more than once again in this chapter. A possible explanation might be the other common material that Matthew and Luke used in addition to Mark, each evangelist combining passages from their sources in different ways.

A second conception of the parables is found in Mark 4:10–12. When they were alone, "those around Jesus" ask him about the parables. Jesus replied that the mystery of the kingdom of God had been given to them, that is, to those who asked, but that to those outside of this intimate circle everything was given in parables. "To you the mystery of the kingdom of God is revealed; to those outside everything comes in parables." What is remarkable is Jesus' addition that this was done so that even if those outside looked keenly they would not see, and if they listened carefully they would not understand, in order to prevent them from repenting and finding forgiveness, "in order that looking keenly they will not see, and listening intently they will not understand, lest they repent and be forgiven." The parables were not told to convey the meaning of the kingdom of God, but to conceal it.

Mark probably understood the saying less radically, taking it in the sense of the mystery of the kingdom of God being disclosed to the intimate circle around Jesus but given to those outside that circle only in the veiled form of parables. Only after the resurrection would the full truth of the kingdom be revealed to all, as we indicated above in chapter 3 on Peter's confession and the predictions of the passion. However, the use of Isaiah 6:9 reveals that the tradition Mark quoted had a more radical meaning; by means of the parables the mystery of the kingdom of God was kept from those outside *so that* no matter how hard they tried, they would not be able to discover it, "*lest* they convert and be forgiven."

The revisions that Matthew introduced into his version of this saying show that he too understood Mark's text in this extremely harsh sense and therefore revised it. To begin with, he changed Mark's "to you the mystery of the kingdom has been given" into "to you it has been given to know the mystery," shifting the emphasis from the fact of the mystery of the kingdom to knowledge about it. It was not the mystery of the kingdom itself that was withheld from the others, but an understanding of it. To explain this further, Matthew used a saying that Mark, followed by Luke, quoted later in the chapter (Matt. 13:12, cf. Mark 4:25, //): whoever shows insight grows in understanding, but the person who is stubborn becomes more and more ignorant of the truth. Matthew used the saying to explain Jesus' use of parables. Through them the difference between those who understood and those who did not manifested itself. (Matthew and Luke each quote this saying once more in different versions and at different locations in their respective Gospels—Matt. 25:29 and Luke 19:26.)

Matthew's most incisive operation was to change Mark's "so that" to "because" in introducing the quoting of Isaiah 6:9 (v. 13) and to eliminate the part of the quotation that reads, "Lest they convert and be forgiven." Compare verse 13 with Mark 4:12. In this way he eliminated the understanding that the parables were intended to *prevent* those outside from understanding; rather they were told *because* of the people's stubbornness. He reinforced this by quoting a larger portion of Isaiah 6, which emphasizes the people's unresponsiveness (vv. 14–15). According to Matthew's version it was the people's close-mindedness that prevented them from understanding the parables. Thus he also altered Mark's more general question concerning the meaning of the parables, "They asked him about the parables" (Mark 4:10), into the specific question, "Why do you speak to them in parables?" (Matt. 13:10). According to Matthew the disciples did not need to ask about the meaning of this or any other parable because, in contrast with those outside, they already understood them. What they wanted to know was why Jesus told parables to those outside. Matthew concluded this part of the chapter with an independent saying that commends the understanding of the disciples (vv. 16–17), in that way reinforcing his more positive tone. Luke has the same saying later in his Gospel (10:23–24).

In this section Luke once more agrees with Matthew against Mark in a number of respects, for instance, in the formulation "to you it is given to know the mysteries of the kingdom [of God]" (8:10). In others he agrees with Mark against Matthew, for example, in introducing the quotation from Isaiah 6:9 with "so that" (v. 10b) in contrast with Matthew's "because." In only one instance does Matthew agree with Mark against Luke: they both have "to those" (Matt. 13:11, Mark 4:11) over and against Luke's "to the others" (Luke 8:10). (This is not recognizable in the RSV, which has "to them" in Matt. 13:11.) Once more it appears that Matthew and Luke depended in part on Mark and in part on another common source. The common quotation of the saying that Matthew has in 13:16–17 and Luke places in a different context in 10:23–24 reveals once more that Matthew and Luke used common material other than Mark.

A third conception of the meaning of the parables is given with the interpretation of the parable of the sower (Mark 4:13–20). Our concern here is not with the interpretation as such but with the fact that an interpretation is given. The interpretation is allegorical, that is, it assumes that parables convey other meanings than that of the stories themselves. For example, in the parable of the sower, what happened to the seeds is not told as an agricultural matter but to express the different ways in which people react to the proclamation of the word. The allegorical interpretation assumes that one needs a key to the story that is told in order to unlock its intended meaning. Although Jesus provided the interpretation in Mark 4:14–20, //s, he chided those who asked him about it for not having recognized the (allegorical) meaning themselves (v. 13).

The interpretation of the parable of the sower is given in response to the request in verse 10 by those around Jesus for a clarification of the parable, and it originally probably followed directly on the request. Jesus' reprimand of the disciples confirms this. Verses 11–12 were evidently interpolated, probably by Mark himself, as a way of introducing his conception of the mystery of the kingdom of God into the discussion of the interpretation of the parables. Note, however, that the present form of the request in verse 10 concerns the parables in general, whereas the reply of Jesus in verses 13–20 presupposes a question concerning specifically the parable of the sower, "You did not understand this parable?!" (v. 13). Mark probably changed the specific question about "this parable" to the general one concerning "the parables" as an adaptation to the saying about the parables in general in verses 11–12. "With the twelve" in verse 10 is easily recognizable as an insertion to draw attention to the presence of the twelve. Luke evidently recognized that the question must have concerned specifically the parable of the sower; he reformulated the question, "What is this parable" (v. 9).

Matthew, as we have noted, even more fundamentally altered the point of the question "why do you speak to them in parables?" (v. 10). According to his understanding, the disciples did not need to ask for an interpretation of the parables because they already understood them. So his introduction to the interpretation of the parable of the sower in verse 18 also does not presuppose a request for clarification of the meaning of the parable. Jesus offered the interpretation on his own initiative as a confirmation of the understanding they already had: "You, thus, have heard [that is, understood] the parable." Matthew similarly left out the chiding of the disciples for not understanding the parable. Luke also omitted the chiding (cf. Luke 8:11) but for different reasons, since he has the disciples ask specifically, "What is [the meaning of] this parable?" (v. 9).

Finally, in Mark 4:33–34 two conceptions of the meaning of the parables come to expression. First, verse 33 states that Jesus "spoke the word to them in many such parables as they were able to understand [literally "hear"]," but then, in verse 34, that "privately he solved everything for his disciples." It almost seems as if the others did not need solutions because the parables were formulated in accordance with their level of understanding (v. 33), but that the disciples needed special instruction (v. 34). In reality the two statements probably represent different traditions, reflecting different conceptions of the parables. According to the statement in verse 33, parables were an effective means of communication, which did not depend on a high level of comprehension from the hearers. Parables were means of instruction for ordinary people. The statement in verse 34, however, interprets the parables as esoteric instruction for a select group. As such they constantly required special interpretation, and Jesus solved the parables for his disciples as a matter of curse.

Mark probably understood the combination of the two sayings as showing that the mystery of the kingdom of God came to those outside only in the veiled form of the parables (v. 33) but was then privately unveiled before the inner group of Jesus' followers (v. 34).

Matthew eliminated two crucial phrases, "As they were able to understand," probably because in his time the parables remained beyond the crowds' ability to understand, and "Privately he solved everything for the disciples," because he did not believe that the disciples needed special instruction to clarify the meaning of the parables. Such ignorance was precisely what distinguished those outside from the disciples, as we have seen above in the discussion of verses 11–15. Luke has no parallel for these verses.

On the basis of the above analysis it becomes possible to distinguish three conceptions of the parables, which probably represent three phases in the development of the tradition.

First, parables are an effective means of communication, which take into account a very general ability to comprehend on the part of the hearers. This conception comes to expression most clearly in the statement that Jesus "spoke the word to them in many such parables *as they were able to understand* (Mark 4:33). It is also assumed in the statement that concludes the parable of the sower, "Whoever has ears to hear, let him/her hear" (Mark 4:9, //s).

Second, parables are intended, not to convey, but to conceal the mystery of the kingdom of God from those who do not belong to the circle of Jesus' followers. As such parables are not intended for the disciples' instruction but for those from whom the mystery of the kingdom is concealed. This conception is represented most clearly by the tradition of Mark 4:11–12, "To those outside everything comes in parables, so that even if they looked keenly they would not see, and if they listened carefully they would not understand." As we have seen, Mark probably understood it in his own sense of the mystery of the kingdom of God, that is, of the parables as the veiled way in which the kingdom of God was proclaimed to those who did not belong to the intimate circle of Jesus' followers.

A third conception of the parables is that they were riddles in need of solutions. There are three slightly different formulations of this conception. (1) According to Mark 4:34, Jesus gave the solutions for these riddles to the disciples when they were alone as a matter of course. (2) In his response to the request for a clarification of the parable of the sower, Jesus chides the disciples for not being able to find the solution themselves: "You do not understand this parable? And how will you understand all the parables?" (Mark 4:13). The expectation is that they themselves should be able to find the solution. (3) This conception is then taken a step further by Matthew, who assumes that the disciples themselves did grasp the meaning of the parables and that Jesus' interpretation of the parable of the sower was merely a confirmation of their understanding: "You have [of course] understood the parable of the sower" (Matt. 13:18). According to Matthew, those who already possessed insight into the parables because of their openness grew in their understanding, whereas those outside the circle of disciples, lacking understanding because of their stubbornness, became increasingly confused. To those who show understanding more will be added so that they will have in abundance, but those who show lack of understanding will grow in their confusion (Matt. 13:12). Matthew's presentation of the traditions concerning the meaning of the parables has become completely consistent, in contrast with Mark, who preserved the conflicting conceptions almost unchanged. With remarkable editorial skill, Matthew eliminated the contradictions between the conflicting formulations with a minimum of alteration.

In these three conceptions of the parables we may be able to recognize three phases in the development of the tradition. The first represents the original phase in which parables were used to illustrate or highlight a point. Contrary to requiring an interpretation, a parable was itself a form of interpretation. Its meaning was not inherent in the story itself but in its use to make or clarify a point. In order to understand a parable in this phase, it was necessary to be familiar with the situation in which it was told. If one knew the situation it would not have been difficult to grasp the point that the parable was making. For example, as we will see in connection with the parable of the banquet (Matt. 22:1–14, //), if Jesus had been challenged because he had table fellowship with publicans and sinners, the parable of the banquet would have been an effective answer. According to the parable, when the dignitaries for whom the banquet had been intended refused to come, the host decided to invite whoever could be found in the streets to sit in their place at his table. The point would have been immediately clear: the religious and social elite in Israel had not responded to God's call and should not now complain when publicans and sinners do respond. Let whoever has ears take note!

Second, with the birth of Christianity, emphasis shifted from the coming of the kingdom of God, which Jesus proclaimed, to Jesus himself as the one through whom God brought salvation to his people. With that shift the original situations in which the parables were told were lost sight of and the parables became incomprehensible, even though they were probably still told as stories that had their own appeal. The new focus on the person of Jesus made the parables confusing because it was not clear what they had to do with the proclamation of salvation in Christ Jesus. The extreme interpretation of them was that they were not intended to communicate that proclamation but were told to prevent those who did not accept Jesus as the savior from discovering the mystery of the kingdom, the death of Jesus as the event of salvation. This stage is represented by the second conception of the meaning of the parables discussed above, as expressed in the tradition of Mark 4:11–12.

Third, in due course, however, what is known as an allegorical interpretation of the parables developed. New meaning was discovered in the parables by looking not to the stories themselves, but to other meanings that were concealed in the parables. The story of the sower whose seeds fell in a variety of places and therefore grew in a variety of ways (Mark 4:1–9, //s) did not really concern the sower and his seed, but in a veiled form told another story, the proclamation of the word of God and various hearers' reaction to it. Verses 4:13–20, //s provides an explanation of that allegorical meaning.

It appears that the allegorical interpretation itself went through several stages represented by the three slightly different conceptions of the parables as riddles in need of solutions, discussed above. (1) In the beginning it was probably necessary for those who first discovered the allegorical meanings to enlighten on a more or less regular basis others who were less insightful. It was assumed that Jesus had done the same for the circle of his disciples, as in Mark 4:34. (2) At a later stage, however, it was assumed that all Christians should be able to discover these meanings for themselves, even though instruction appears still to have been given where it was called for. This stage is represented by the saying in Mark 4:13, in which Jesus chides the disciples for not understanding the parable of the sower. The disciples in the Gospel of Mark are presented as having comprehended very little about Jesus. Here the emphasis is on their inability to find the allegorical meaning of the parables for themselves. (3) Finally, at the stage of Matthew's version of the tradition, it had become possible to assume that the allegorical meanings were recognizable by all or at least by those who were in the inner circle of the Christian community. When the allegorical meaning was nevertheless given, it was done more or less as a confirmation of an already recognized meaning, not as instruction, as in Matthew's introduction to the allegorical interpretation of the parable of the sower.

We may assume that not all the parables that were handed down in primitive Christianity came from Jesus. The New Testament Church had neither the developed critical ability nor the tools and information with which to distinguish between sayings that came from Jesus and those that did not. Actually, we are equally incapable of doing so because even though we do have a developed critical ability, we have even less information, which renders our critical tools inadequate for the task of making such distinctions. In addition to the probable presence of parables that did not originate from Jesus but became part of the tradition about him because they expressed a similar meaning to what they remembered of him, others were almost certainly developed in the Christian communities themselves. A probable candidate for such an early Christian product is the so-called parable of the tares (Matt. 13:24–30), for which an allegorical interpretation is given in Matthew 13:36–43. Notwithstanding the attempts of New Testament scholars to find an original parable behind the present version of the story in verses 24–30, its most probable meaning remains the allegorical interpretation given in verses 36–43. The story was probably told from the beginning with the allegorical meaning in mind. The story itself should thus be recognized as an allegory and should not be taken as a parable.

An allegory—or an allegorical interpretation—does not have to be inferior. The allegory of the tares has a very important message. When it became clear that the church was a mixed body that included not only people who were true to the Christian calling but also others who were unworthy of it, if not outright impostors, some members of the Christian community wanted to take it upon themselves to separate out the unworthy. (Paul does so in a single case involving immorality in 1 Cor. 5:1–5). In that situation the allegory of the tares presents a sober message: "By gathering the weeds you may also uproot the wheat" (v. 29). The task of separating the weeds (tares) from the wheat, the goats from the sheep, should be left to God himself and his angels, who will do so on the day of judgment (v. 30, cf. vv. 39b–43).

In the case of the parables, like that of the beatitudes, Jesus' influence on the early Christian community was not limited to those parables for which Jesus himself was responsible, nor were their meanings limited to their original significance. His influence was felt forcefully as Christians tried to cope with new situations, which they interpreted by using the parables or by producing new parables or allegories in the tradition of Jesus. Sometimes they gave new interpretations to existing parables—as we will see in the parable of the banquet.

2. THE PARABLE OF THE BANQUET (MATT. 22:1–14, //; #279)

The two versions of this parable in Matthew and in Luke have few verbal formulations in common. The evangelists evidently did not copy from a single source. Nevertheless, it is not difficult to recognize that they do have two versions of the same story. There is yet another version of it in the Gospel of Thomas (saying 64), to which we will refer only in passing.

This story also has an interesting rabbinic parallel. A pious student of the Law and the son of the publican Ma'jan died at approximately the same time. The student had a burial of which no one took notice, whereas the whole town stopped working to honor the deceased son of the publican. This apparent inequity distressed a fellow student of the Law, who, however, received a vision in a dream revealing the true nature of the situation. The pious student had committed a very small transgression—he had once put on his head **phylactery** before his hand phylactery—and in order to ensure his perfect bliss in the other world, God allowed his burial to go unnoticed as an atonement for his transgression. The son of Ma'jan, however, even though he was an unrighteous man, performed a good deed shortly before his death, and in order to avoid any outstanding merits for which compensation would be due him in the other world, God allowed him to be honored so highly at his funeral. The good deed of the publican's son was that he had arranged a banquet for the city councilors, and when they did not come, he had his servants invite the poor from the streets to eat the food that had been prepared to prevent it from going to waste. (Others said that at the market a beggar picked up a loaf of bread that had fallen from his basket and he did not try to stop him because that would have been undignified.) In a second vision, a few days later, the surviving student saw the student who had died enjoying perfect bliss in the other world, whereas the son of Ma'jan was unsuccessfully trying to lap up water from a stream (Palestinian Talmud, *Sanhedrin* 6:23c = *Chagiga* 2:77d). It is evident that the story of someone inviting the poor to a banquet to which the guests who were originally invited refused to come was known outside Christian circles.

In the case of the two versions of the parable in the Gospels it is possible to uncover the common tradition on which they were based by listing the differences between them and eliminating what appear to be interpretive features. The following differences between the two versions can be noted:

1. In Matthew the connection to the kingdom of God is established with the usual formula with which most of the parables are introduced in the Gospels: "The kingdom of God is like a king" (v. 2). The intention is not to equate the kingdom of God with the king who gives the wedding feast for his son; what is meant is that the situation with regard to the kingdom of God is similar to that of a king giving a wedding feast for his son. In Luke the connection is established only circumstantially. Someone in the company of Jesus says, "Blessed is whoever eats bread in the kingdom of God" (v. 15), to which Jesus responds with the parable. The parable in Luke should thus be understood within the context of the saying about eating bread in the kingdom of God.

2. In Matthew it is a king who gives a marriage feast for his son (v. 2), whereas in Luke it is merely "some person" who gives a banquet (v. 16).

3. In Matthew a group of servants is sent twice to invite the guests (vv. 3–4), whereas in Luke a single servant is sent only once (v. 17).

4. In Matthew the second group of servants is mistreated, some of them even killed (v. 6). Nothing similar happens in Luke.

5. In Matthew the guests' refusal to accept the invitation is stated very briefly (v. 5), whereas their excuses are elaborated in Luke (vv. 18–20).

6. In Matthew the king sends his armies to destroy the city of his servants' murderers (v. 7). Luke has nothing parallel.

7. Matthew has only one subsequent invitation to the people from the streets (vv. 89–90), whereas Luke includes two subsequent invita-

tions, first to people in the streets of the city (v. 21), and then to those on the country roads (vv. 22–23).

8. Matthew emphasizes that both the good and the bad were invited (v. 10); according to Luke the host merely states, "Induce them to come in, so that my house will be full" (v. 23).

9. Luke concludes the parable with the statement that none of the original guests would be allowed to participate in the banquet (v. 24), whereas Matthew includes an additional scene in which the king appears at the banquet and, finding a guest without a wedding garment, has him thrown out (vv. 11–13). Matthew concludes the story with the saying that many are called but few elected (v. 14).

The difference in the introductions to the two versions of the parable is of little significance. Both indicate that the parable concerns participation in the kingdom of God, Matthew directly and Luke by means of the statement to which it is a response.

Matthew's elaboration of the host as a king giving a wedding feast for his son, however, is obviously an allegorizing interpretation. The king is God, the son is Christ, and the wedding feast is the messianic banquet in the kingdom of God. Similarly, Matthew's two invitations through more than one servant appear to be an elaboration when compared with Luke. The Gospel of Thomas also has only one servant who is sent only once. The mistreatment and murder of the second group of servants in Matthew, which the king avenges with the destruction of the murderers' city, almost certainly refers to the mistreating and killing of Christian leaders, for example, Stephen (Acts 7:54–60) and James (Acts 12:2), and to the destruction of Jerusalem in A.D. 70 as God's punishment for these acts. The two invitations through more than one servant may distinguish between the earlier activity of the prophets and the subsequent mission of Christian evangelists.

Luke's more elaborate excuses do not appear to have allegorical significance; they merely function as storytelling embellishments. In the Gospel of Thomas the refusals are similarly elaborated. Repeated elaborations are not uncommon in parables, for example, in the parable of the sower (cf. Mark 4:4–7, //s), and in the parable of Jotham in Judges 9:7–21, where the trees successively ask the olive, the fig tree, and the vine to reign as king over them, with repeated refusals (vv. 8–13), until the bramble finally agrees (vv. 14–15). The fact that Luke has two subsequent invitations, however, may be an allegorization of the Christian mission, first to the underprivileged among the Jews (inside the city walls) and then to the Gentiles (those on the country roads).

The intention of Matthew's emphasis that both the good and the bad be brought in (v. 10) is not immediately evident. Through the scene with the man without a wedding garment, however, it becomes clear that it refers to the fact that in Matthew's own time the church was composed of both steadfast and unfaithful members, as in his allegory of the tares (13:24–

30, #127, cf. 36–43, #131). This understanding is confirmed by the saying with which he concludes the story, "Many are called [into the church], but few are [worthy of being] elected for the kingdom of God" (v. 14).

Luke's statement that persons should even be forced to come in so that the host's house would be filled may be based on the eschatological conception of the "fullness," that is, the rounding off of a fixed number of persons before the end could come. We see this, for example, in Romans 11:25, where Paul unveils the mystery that "the hardening of Israel was in part [to provide time] until the fullness of the Gentiles could enter," or in Revelation 6:11 in the reply to the souls under the altar who cry out to know how long it is going to be before God takes revenge on those who were responsible for the shedding of their blood; "They should be patient for a while yet, until the number has become full of their fellow servants and brothers who were to be murdered like them." It is possible, however, that Luke's statement could have been purely a feature of the story itself, expressing the host's generosity and his joy in the anticipation of seeing his house full.

Matthew concludes his parable with a scene in which a person who is found without a wedding garment is cast out. The scene raises the difficulty that one would not expect of the persons who were called in from the streets to have been dressed for a wedding; a person who was not appropriately dressed could hardly have been an exception. The two parts of the story do not fit together very well. Rabbinic tradition includes a parallel that sheds light on the incident with the wedding garment in the second part of the story. According to the tractate on the Sabbath, Rabbi Eliezer, who lived at the end of the first century, taught that one should repent on the day before one's death. When his students asked him how one could know the day on which one was to die, he replied that one should repent every day since one could die on the next, and so one's entire life should be spent in repentance. His answer is substantiated by reference to Rabbi Jochannan ben Zakkai's interpretation of Ecclesiastes 9:8: "Let your clothing always be white, and let oil never be missing from your forehead." According to Rabbi Jochannan, who lived at the end of the first century, the saying meant obedience to the commandments, good works, and study of the Law. His interpretation was in turn explained with the following story: A king invited his subjects to a feast but did not let them know the time. The wise among his subjects went ahead and prepared themselves for the feast. They put on clean clothes and waited at the door of the palace, saying to themselves, "In palaces everything is available in abundance; it would be possible to have the feast anytime." The foolish, however, thought that a great effort would be needed to prepare the feast, and so each went to his or her work. When the feast was announced the wise were ready, but the foolish appeared in their dirty work clothes. This angered the king very much. However, he did not send them away, but as punishment he tormented them by having them stand and watch the others eat (Tractate Sabbath 153a).

Matthew evidently added to the parable of the banquet a concluding scene that was originally a separate story. The rabbinic parallel clarifies its point, which was that one should always be ready for the day of judgment in order not to be caught unprepared. The man without a wedding garment symbolized his unpreparedness for the day of judgment, which caught him unprepared.

This confirms our suggestion earlier of what Matthew meant when he stated that both the good and the bad should be invited (v. 10). Both steadfast and unfaithful persons were included in the church, but when God came in judgment he would separate the bad from the good. Matthew has abandoned the framework of the story of the royal feast for that of its (allegorical) meaning when he formulates the king's command to his servants, "Tie his feet and hands and throw him into the most remote darkness. There will be moaning and gnashing of teeth" (v. 13). Matthew is no longer talking allegorically about a king who appears at a wedding feast but directly about God's eschatological judgment.

In Matthew's version of the parable we thus have an allegory of the church. It symbolizes the festive gathering at the marriage feast that God prepared for his son. The history of its realization includes the work of the prophets and Christian evangelists whose invitations were rejected by Israel. They were met with hostility and some of them were even murdered, an act for which God punished Israel with the destruction of Jerusalem by the Roman armies. Because of Israel's rejection of the invitation to accept Christ, it was extended to others who did accept and so constituted the church as the true Israel. Matthew knew, however, as he made clear with the allegory of the tares (Matt. 13:24–30, cf. 36–43), that the church was constituted, not only by those who were true to the Christian calling, but also by those who were unworthy of it. It is with that in mind that he added the story of the man without a wedding garment as a warning to remain prepared.

The allegorical retelling of the parable in this extended form is not merely a history of the coming into being of the church but also a warning for Christians not to take membership in the believing community as a guarantee of salvation. No one had grounds to feel secure when compared with Israel, unless she or he behaved in an appropriate way. In the discussion of the last judgment below, we will see more clearly what Matthew meant by that. It is sufficient at this stage to quote his saying in 7:21, "Not everyone who calls me Lord, Lord, will enter into the kingdom of the heavens, but the one who does the will of my father who is in heaven." In this way Matthew's allegorical retelling of the parable of the banquet and the man without a wedding garment gives new meaning to these stories as they were handed down in the primitive church.

Luke's allegorization is less apparent and not as complete as Matthew's but nevertheless present. He too tells the parable as an allegory of the history of the church but with a different focus. The church is the haven for the socially and the religiously underprivileged, represented by, on the one hand, the unfortunate in Israel, "Bring in the poor, the maimed, the blind, and the lame" (v. 21), and, on the other, by the Gentiles, "Go out on the roads and the alleys and make them come in" (v. 23). Together they constitute the church as the new Israel. Luke's conclusion about the Jews is harsh and as vengeful as Matthew's reference to the destruction of Jerusalem, "Not one of those persons who were invited [originally] will sit at my table" (v. 24). It reflects the extreme bitterness that had developed between Jews and the growing Christian religion.

Behind these two versions of the parable we can recognize a still simpler one on which both depended. A man gives a banquet, but the invited guests decline to come, so he sends his servant to the streets to invite all whom they could find to sit at his table. It is similar to the story of the son of Ma'jan, but it probably made a different point in a different situation. The context in which a parable is told is what determines its point. Jesus could have told the parable as yet another justification for his table fellowship with publicans and sinners by illustrating it with the parable. The parable presents a similar situation as that to which his questioners referred. As John the Baptist had warned, "Do not think you can say to yourself, 'We have our father Abraham.' I say to you that God can raise children for himself from these stones" (Matt. 3:9, //).

The lack of verbal similarity in Matthew's and Luke's telling of the story, coupled with the existence of a rabbinic version, makes it unlikely that Matthew and Luke quoted the story from a common source. At the same time, the existence of yet another Christian version of it in the Gospel of Thomas (saying 64) reveals that the parable was well established in the Christian tradition. The version of the parable in Thomas is even less allegorical than in Luke: A man prepares a banquet, and when he sends his servants to summon the guests, they respond with four different excuses (compared with Luke's three). Thereupon the man sends his servant to go to the streets to invite whomever he can find. There is no hint at allegorization. The "saying" ends with the somewhat artificial conclusion, "The buyers and the merchants [shall] not [come] into the places of my [i.e. , Jesus'] Father," which interprets it as an example story, illustrating the harmful effects of the occupations of buyers and merchants.

Conclusion. In the tradition of the parables, as in that of the beatitudes and other sayings of Jesus, New Testament Christianity did not merely hand down what they believed to have been said by Jesus. Rather, they interpreted these traditions, continually adapting them to new situations. In that way they kept them alive, finding new meanings for the traditions about Jesus in constantly changing situations.

C. CHRISTIANITY BEYOND CONFESSION
(MATT. 25:31–46; #300)

The description of the last judgment begins on a grand apocalyptic scale. The Son of Man, accompanied by a host of angels, arrives and seats himself on a glorious throne, and all he peoples of the earth are brought before him to be judged. He separates the good from the evil as a shepherd separates goats form sheep, sheep on the right and goats on the left (vv. 31–33).

But then without notice the scene changes. It is no longer the grand apocalyptic scene with the Son of Man but a king explaining to those who had just been judged on what grounds the judgment had been made—simply whether or not they cared for the needy. The most significant feature of this clarification is that care for those who are hungry, thirsty, strangers, naked, sick, or in prison is equated with care for the king himself. It is again possible to refer to a rabbinic parallel. In a Jewish commentary on Deuteronomy 15:9, God says to Israel, "My children, when you give the poor to eat, I reckon it to you as if you had given me to eat." (*Midrash Tannaim* on Deut. 15:9). Indeed, if only two phrases in the second part of Matthew's description were eliminated, " of my father" in verse 34 and "my brothers" in verse 40, nothing would be left to identify it as specifically Christian. Neither of these phrases is essential to the passage; without them the description could have been a Jewish story used here to interpret the basis on which the judgment in the first part of the description was made. The two parts evidently did not belong together originally. This is clearly shown by the change in nomenclature for the judge, "Son of Man" in the first part and a "king" in the second. The first part can be taken as complete in itself. It presents the awesome reality of a final judgment, as in the closing scene of Matthew's version of the parable of the banquet (22:11–13) and in the allegory of the tares (13:24–30, cf. 36–43), specifically in the statement of verses 41–42, "The Son of Man will send his angels, and they will gather from his kingdom all the stumbling blocks and those who did evil and will throw them into the furnace."

As an interpretation of the grounds on which the Son of Man separated the good and the evil in verses 32–33 of the present passage, the second scene is a clarification of what it means to confess Jesus. It was by their actions that both those who took care of the needy and those who did not acknowledged or denied Jesus, even though neither group had been aware of it. The situation described in Luke 12:8–9 remains true: "Everyone who acknowledges me before people the Son of Man will acknowledge before the angels of God" (cf. Matt. 10:32–33). What has changed is that acknowledgment or denial of Jesus is no longer understood as the public confession or denial of him, but as something that takes place in the acts of aiding or ignoring the needy.

There is, of course, moral value in the actions of those who aid the needy. In that regard the description makes the same point as the Jewish commentary on Deutoronomy 15:9. But in our passage a principle of even greater significance is involved. It does not merely lay down a moral principle but uses that principle to interpret what it means to confess or deny Jesus. Confession or denial of him is not what motivated the actions of those who cared and those who did not care for the needy—neither of the groups were aware that Christ had been involved—but their caring for the needy or failure to do so amounted to confessing or denying Christ. In other words, it was not that religious motivation determined the moral value of their actions but, inversely, that the moral value of their actions made them religiously significant. In this passage we find confirmation that it is not of fundamental significance whether Jesus developed the conviction that the kingdom of God had already come to justify his behavior or whether that conviction actually motivated his behavior. Whatever the case may have been, by interpreting his fellowship with publicans and sinners within the framework of the coming of the kingdom of God, Jesus claimed fundamental religious significance for his behavior. In the description of the last judgment, Matthew claims that behavior similar to that of Jesus, recognizing the human dignity of those who do not count—morally, socially, and religiously—and behaving toward them with respect for that dignity is what it means to confess Jesus.

Conclusion. In the first part of this study we concluded that the significance of Jesus was not to be found in her person but in the way in which he pointed to John the Baptist as the justification for his behavior. John's activity marked the transition from the previous age of expectation to the time of the kingdom of God, and because the kingdom of God had come, Jesus was justified in associating with those who did not count religiously, socially, and morally, proclaiming the good tidings of the coming of the kingdom to them and making them his friends. Jesus claimed that his behavior was justified by the activity of John, by the fact that John's expectation of the coming of the kingdom of God had been fulfilled, inaugurated by John's own activity as the returning Elijah. There is thus truth in Matthias Grünewald's famous painting in which John points his elongated forefinger to Jesus as the one who was to come. However, the full reality of who Jesus was is recognized only if one pictures also the inverse of the painting, Jesus pointing to the one who marked the transition between the ages. John's activity was Jesus' justification for his own behavior, as expressed in the traditions of Matthew 11:2–19, //s and especially in Mark 11:27–30, where he explicitly states that John's activity is the framework within which the authority for his own work is located. In that way he claimed fundamental religious significance for what he did.

Within the course of Jesus' own life emphasis had already shifted from his activity to his person. What we do not know is whether Jesus himself played a part in encouraging such a shift. That it did occur is attested to by the fact that some of his followers thought of him as the messiah who was to liberate the Jewish people from Roman rule. The stories of his entry into Jerusalem and of the cleansing of the temple make it impossible to reject with certainty that he himself may have encouraged such an understanding. Whatever may have happened during his lifetime, it was his death and his followers' efforts to cope with it, that brought his person into central focus, in their belief in his resurrection, his sitting at the right hand of God, and his expected return as the Son of Man.

New Testament Christianity, however, did not lose itself completely in the worship of Jesus as a heavenly being. Believers also preserved traditions about his earthly existence. These traditions were reinterpreted and expanded as they were handed down to adapt them to changing circumstances. Traditions from other sources were almost certainly added, and new ones originated in the New Testament Christian communities themselves. Nevertheless, a large share of the original image was preserved and remained determinative for the character of what became the Jesus tradition.

In Matthew's description of the last judgment the original emphasis on the activity of Jesus reasserted itself against the focus on his person. This return to the original emphasis is formulated succinctly in the statement that "not everyone who calls me Lord, Lord, will enter into the kingdom of God, but the person who does the will of my father who is in the heavens" (Matt. 7:21).

With this interpretation of what it means to confess Jesus, Christianity not only returned to its roots in the behavior of Jesus; it also affirmed the priority of his activity over and against the interpretation given to it. In the first part of our study we left only partly resolved the problem whether Jesus' behavior was motivated by his conviction that John's activity had ushered in the kingdom of God, or whether he developed that conviction as a way of justifying his behavior. We concluded that in the final analysis it does not really matter which came first; what does matter was that by interpreting his behavior within the framework of John's inauguration of the kingdom of God, Jesus claimed fundamental religious significance for it. In so doing he rejected the interpretation of his behavior as an arbitrary whim, even if that may have been its initial motivation. Out of his outrageous behavior—the harsh rejection of his relatives in favor of the publicans and sinners around him—emerged the most fundamental principle of Christianity, behavior grounded in recognition of the fundamental human dignity of also those who do not count religiously, socially, and morally.

Matthew's description of the last judgment does not resolve the historical question of which came first, Jesus' scandalous behavior or his conviction that the kingdom of God had arrived, but it does answer the question of the principle involved, the affirmation of the priority of his behavior. The ultimate religious significance attached to the actions of those who took care of the needy and of those who did not is not the motivation for their behavior, but the affirmation of it. In Romans, Paul established a principle that further radicalized Matthew's interpretation. He wrote, "Not the person who proclaims it publicly is a Jew, and neither is what is performed in the flesh circumcision, but [the person who acts without making religious claims for what she or he does] is a Jew, and circumcision is of the heart, in the spirit and not in the flesh" (2:28–29). What he meant is that "not those who hear the Law are justified before God, but those who do what the Law requires will be justified" (2:13).

The same principle should apply to what it means to be a Christian. "Not the person who proclaims it publicly is a Christian, and neither is what is professed publicly confession, but the person who behaves in a certain way without making religious claims for his or her behavior is a Christian, and confession is of the heart, in what one does and not in what one says."

In his description of the last judgment Matthew points out the behavior through which the confession of Jesus is made, and in so doing he points back to Jesus. It does not matter how one interprets the behavior, whether Christian (as in Matthew's description), or Jewish (as in the Jewish commentary on Deut. 15:9), or whether one interprets it at all. It is the behavior itself that counts; whatever distinctions exist are attributable to the interpretations. Jesus' recognition of the importance of this behavior may have been his greatest contribution. He interpreted John's deeply religious activity and his own irreverence for the social, moral, and religious distinctions as grounded in the same authority (Mark 11:27–33, cf. Matt. 11:18–19), claiming that the kingdom of God was already present, not in the desert, the traditional place for the meeting with God where John prepared for it, but in the place where the needs of those who suffered were met (Matt. 11:5). It now becomes clear that in so doing Jesus not only justified his own behavior (Matt. 11:6) but also interpreted the deeply religious concerns of his teacher in terms of the alleviation of human suffering as prophesied by Isaiah (Matt. 11:5).

Matthew returned to the same fundamental position when he interpreted the confession of faith in Jesus in terms of care for the needy. In that way he gave recognition to the concern for human suffering as a cardinal principle of Christianity. The ultimate meaning of being a Christian was not the public confession of Jesus but the affirmation of him by recognizing, as he did, the human dignity of those who did not count from a religious, social, and moral point of view.

Glossary

Apocalypticism. Derived from the Greek word for "unveil," the term refers to Jewish religious thinking concerning the unveiling of hidden knowledge. A relevant feature of this thinking for understanding the Jesus movement is the expectation that the present evil age would soon come to an end and be replaced by a new age of the kingdom of God. An example of this kind of thinking is the so-called "Little Apocalypse" in Mark 13, //s.

Eschatology. Derived from the Greek word for "end," the term refers to teachings about the end. In the sense of Jewish expectations in the time of Jesus it refers to events that were to have signaled the end of the present world period and the beginning of the time of the kingdom of God.

Etiological legend. Derived from the Greek word for "cause," the term refers to the explanation of the name or other features of a place, person, etc., by means of a story explaining its origin.

Gospel of Thomas. A collection of 114 sayings of Jesus, which follow each other without connections, most of them beginning simply with "Jesus said." It is part of a Gnostic library that was discovered in Nag Hammadi in Egypt in 1945.

Hellenistic. The culture that emerged after the conquests of Alexander the Great (356–323 B.C.), when Oriental religious thinking was absorbed into Greek of Hellenic culture. There has been a tendency at times to contrast Jewish and Hellenistic thought, but Jewish thinking in New Testament times, which had not escaped Hellenistic influence, was itself a Hellenistic subculture.

Mishnah. Jewish legal interpretations and traditions codified by Rabbi Judah in the second half of the second century A.D., which form the core of the Talmud. It is divided into six orders that are further divided into tractates, such as the tractates *Sanhedrin* and *Sabbath*, referred to in the present volume.

Mystery religions. Secretive cults that thrived all over the Mediterranean world during New Testament times. The most renowned were devoted to the Egyptian deities, Isis and Osiris, to the Persian, Mithras, and the Syrian mother goddess, Kybele, and her consort, Attis. Central to most of these cults was the celebration of the dying and resurrection of the cult deity, symbolizing the return of new life after the winter.

Oxyrhynchus Papyri. Papyrus documents discovered in an excavation site of that name in Upper Egypt, ranging in date from 100 B.C. to the tenth century A.D. They include literary, religious, and legal texts.

Parousia. A Greek term meaning basically "presence," it was used to refer to the arrival, for example, of a king or high official. Paul uses it for Stephen in 1 Corinthians 16:17, for Titus in 2 Corinthians 7:6–7, and for himself in 2 Corinthians 10:10 and Philippians 1:26 and 2:12. In a technical sense in the New Testament it refers to the arrival of Jesus as Son of Man.

Phylactery. Small leather boxes containing passages from Scripture inscribed on parchment, worn by Jews on their foreheads and left hands during prayer.

Pseudo-Clementines. An early Christian romance written in the name of Clement I, describing, among other things, how he became a disciple of the apostle Peter. It is in the form of twenty "homilies" and ten "recognitions" or remembrances.

Sanhedrin. The Jewish high court in Jerusalem, which dealt with matters of religious and civil law. Its construction and procedures is the main topic of the tractate *Sanhedrin* in the Mishnah.

Septuagint. The third century B.C. Greek translation of the Jewish Scriptures by hellenistic Jews. Legend attributes it to seventy-two translators who completed it in seventy-two days for Ptolemy Philadelphus (285–221 B.C.), from where it received the name Septuagint, meaning "seventy." It is abbreviated with the Roman numeral LXX.

Synoptic Gospels. The term used to identify the first three New Testament Gospels because they can be read synoptically when laid side by side.

Targum. An Aramaic word meaning "translation," it refers to a paraphrase translation of the Hebrew Scriptures that was made when Aramaic, a related Semitic language, replaced Hebrew among Palestinian and Babylonian Jews.

Index of Names and Topics

unworthy, 122, 126
uprising, xv, 39, 81, 84–85, 88–93
Uriah, 23

veiled, 116, 119, 121
vicarious, 91, 110
violate, 44, 67, 69, 75
violence, 28, 44, 45, 80, 85

wisdom, 20, 91
wise, 125
witness(es), xvi, 5, 20, 27, 33, 68, 54, 68–70, 72

woe(s), 34–35, 102, 112–13, 115
wordplay, 57
worker(s), 7
worship, 12, 15, 28, 62–63, 88, 99, 130

Zarathustra, 28
Zebedee, 98
Zebulun, 14
Zechariah (father of John the Baptist), 19, 32–33
Zerubbabel, 23

Index of Biblical and Other Ancient Texts